C A V

CAVE ROCK

CLIMBERS, COURTS, AND A WASHOE INDIAN SACRED PLACE

Matthew S. Makley
AND
Michael J. Makley

UNIVERSITY OF NEVADA PRESS
RENO AND LAS VEGAS

University of Nevada Press, Reno, Nevada 89557 USA

Manufactured in the United States of America
Design by Kathleen Szawiola

LIBRARY OF CONGRESS CATALOGING-IN-PUBLICATION DATA
Makley, Matthew S., 1974–
Cave Rock : climbers, courts, and a Washoe Indian sacred place /
Matthew S. Makley and Michael J. Makley.
p. cm.
Includes bibliographical references and index.
ISBN 978-0-87417-827-2 (pbk. : alk. paper)
1. Cave Rock (Nev.) 2. Access Fund—Trials, litigation, etc.
3. United States. Forest Service—Trials, litigation, etc.
4. Washoe Tribe of Nevada and California—Trials, litigation, etc.
5. Washoe Indians—Legal status, laws, etc. 6. Sacred space—
Law and legislation—Nevada. 7. Rock climbing—
Law and legislation—Nevada. I. Makley, Michael J. II. Title.
KF229.A28M35 2010
344.793'099—dc22 2010014695

The paper used in this book is a recycled stock made from
30 percent post-consumer waste materials, certified by
FSC, and meets the requirements of American National
Standard for Information Sciences—Permanence of Paper
for Printed Library Materials, ANSI/NISO Z39.48-1992 (R2002).
Binding materials were selected for strength and durability.

2019 18 17 16 15
10 9 8 7 6 5

FOR THE NEXT GENERATION

Mikiah, Alijah, Charlotte, Dominic, and Olivia

CONTENTS

LIST OF ILLUSTRATIONS

PREFACE

In the late 1990s my son, Matthew, and I became aware of a dispute over one of Lake Tahoe's best-known landmarks: Cave Rock. The clash between Washoe Indians, who held the property sacred, and rock climbers, who used its world-class climbing routes, simmered and periodically boiled until it was resolved by the federal court system in 2007. Throughout the process my interest in documentary filmmaking motivated me to tape interviews with climbers and tribal members. I also recorded four public meetings the U.S. Forest Service called to discuss the use of the site. From the recorded material I produced a thirty-minute video, *Cave Rock: The Issue,* which was subsequently used as a source document in the court cases. When the Ninth Circuit Court of Appeals issued the final verdict in 2007, Matthew and I decided to chronicle the dispute in book form.

Our connection to this topic is personal as well as academic. I lived in South Lake Tahoe, a few miles from Cave Rock, for more than thirty years. I worked seven summer seasons for the Forest Service at Tahoe and maintain friendships with Washoes and Tahoe Basin climbers alike. Matthew grew up in the area and also has friends among both groups. He wrote a Washoe tribal history for his Ph.D. dissertation and now teaches American Indian history at Metro State College in Denver. In the work that follows, he wrote the Washoe parts, and I dealt with the climbing history and court cases.

Writing this book proved to be a fulfilling enterprise, shepherded to its conclusion by Matt "Becks" Becker at the University of Nevada Press. His editorial guidance and suggestions greatly enhanced the work; he has earned our appreciation and gratitude. Others at the press to whom we owe thanks include Director Joanne O'Hare, Managing Editor Sara Vélez Mallea, Design Manager Kathleen Szawiola, and Marketing Manager Barbara Berlin. Marcia Yablon's *Yale Law Journal* paper, cited in the endnotes, provided a significant overview of the complex problems and possible solutions involved in settling Native sacred site claims. Heidi Englund of the Nevada Historical Society helped us to acquire materials on early roads and the tunnels accessing Cave Rock; she also helped us reference historical photographs of the site. Joel Guldner assisted our acquisitions of photos from the University of Nevada, Reno, Special Collections Department. Melinda Conner's workmanship in editing the text was superior. She was exacting and thorough, improving its clarity, readability, and continuity. Matthew wishes to thank Peter Iverson, Donald Fixico, Sherry Smith, Waziyatawin Angela Wilson, Susan Miller, Lisa Emmerich, Michael Magliari, John Yarnevich, Steve Leonard, and Jim Drake. Most of all we express thanks to Alea and Randi for their constant support.

CAVE ROCK

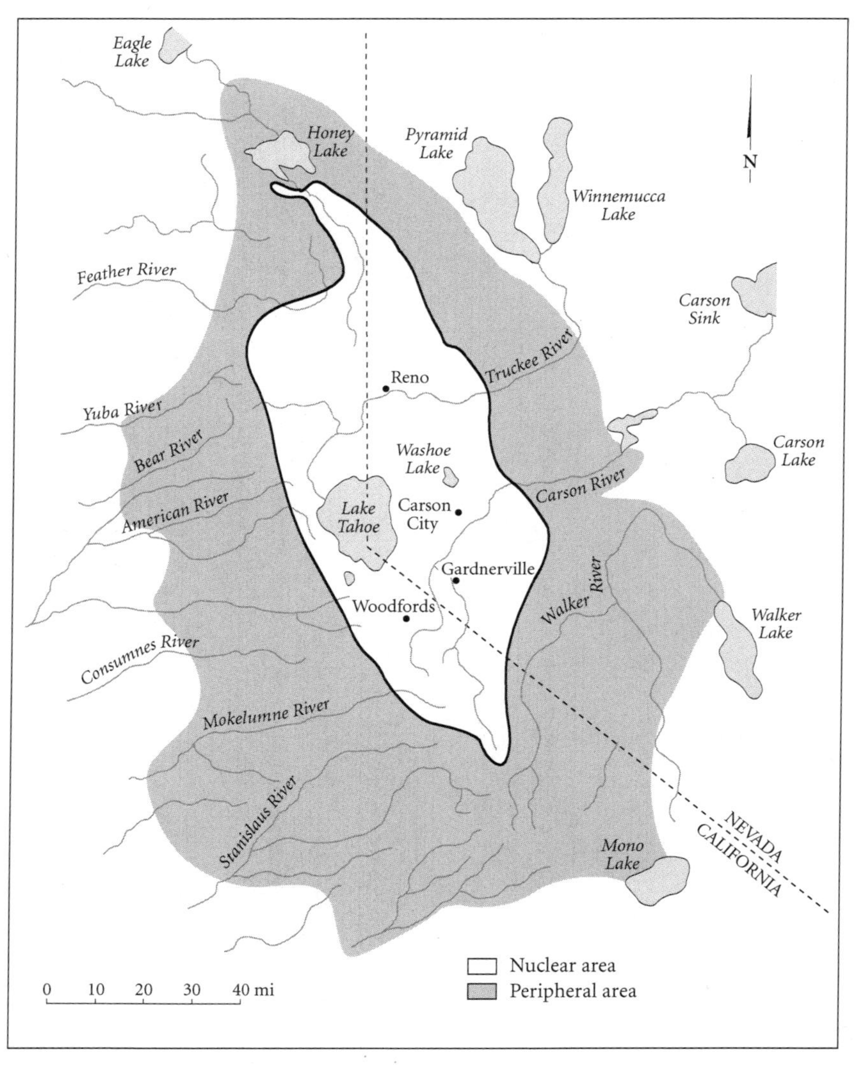

Traditional Washoe homelands. The white "nuclear" area represents lands used on a regular basis where communities kept permanent village sites. Gray "peripheral" areas include extended hunting, gathering, and trading lands. Notice Lake Tahoe in the center. Versions of this map have been used since the boundaries were officially set during the Indian Claims Commission case in 1948.

Introduction

Suddenly it was over. After twenty years filled with bitter disputes, regulatory schizophrenia, and litigation, the U.S. Court of Appeals for the Ninth Circuit had resolved the issue of Cave Rock. On August 27, 2007, the court upheld the U.S. district court's ruling, and rock climbing at the sacred monolith ended. In an unlikely outcome, the Washoe Indians, a community of 1,900 members, defeated the Access Fund, a climbers' advocacy group sponsored by more than one hundred corporations, including giants such as Nike, Microsoft, Charles Schwab, North Face, and REI. The case set a precedent: for the first time, Native American concerns had closed a popular climbing site on federal property.

Lake Tahoe, a pristine body of water that covers 191 square miles in the High Sierra, occupies the center of Washoe ancestral lands. Cave Rock, named De' ek wadapush (Rock Standing Gray) in the Washoe language, dominates Tahoe's eastern shoreline, rising in a 360-foot vertical sweep. The granite mass is the core remnant of a volcano that erupted some three million years ago. During the Pleistocene epoch, with the lake level 150 feet higher than today, wave action formed caves in the rock. The main cave, in the middle of the formation, is eighteen feet wide and ten feet high at its mouth, and extends horizontally thirty feet to its eight-foot-by-eight-foot back wall. At least one observer has compared it to the caves that gave birth to the deities of Mount Olympus.[1]

The granite massif of which the cave is a part comprises approximately two acres, including three hundred feet of shoreline. Early chroniclers described it as half a cathedral dome, and as a jagged promontory rising like a clenched fist. Viewed from the lakeshore below Mount Tallac to the southwest, the mass resembles a sphinx; from Meeks Bay, nine miles directly west across the lake, it appears to be a pyramid surrounding an open vault. The northern view features a fifty-foot silhouette of the "Lady of the Lake" below the main cave. An early photograph taken from the north shows a series of Indian faces profiled in the rock above the Lady.[2]

The Washoe people believe that the waters of Lake Tahoe "breathe life into the land, plants, fish, birds, animals, and people around it." Historically, Cave Rock provided Washoe shamans, or doctors, with the most important source of power in the Tahoe basin. Tribal members continue to believe that proper use of Cave Rock is necessary to maintain the health and welfare of Washoes and non-Washoes alike.[3]

When the Washoes still exercised control over a large expanse of the Sierra from Susanville, California, to Bishop, California, families made a yearly trek to Lake Tahoe in the spring and lived on the lakeshore until late fall, when they returned to their villages in the valleys. Paths circumscribed the lake, but at Cave Rock the only thoroughfare was a narrow deer trail behind it. Traditionally, only Washoe shamans came near the cave, making periodic visits to cultivate power. The community's welfare depended on the success of its healers, and authorization to approach a place of power came from higher sources. Power and the places where it reposed held danger for those not specifically chosen or trained to handle it.[4]

Even as the dominant American majority imposed their culture on the Washoes, traditional practitioners continued to journey to the cave to practice their secret rites. Washoe doctors Welewkushkush; Dick Bagley; Blind Mike Dick; Beleliwe; and the latter's protégé, the renowned Henry Rupert, also known as Moses, utilized the cave in the twentieth century.

Today, many Washoes hold the site so sacrosanct that they will follow a winding, mostly two-lane highway seventy-two miles around the lake to reach nearby destinations rather than drive through the tunnels constructed in the twentieth century below the main cave.[5]

The members of John C. Frémont's expedition in 1844 were the first Euro-Americans to see Lake Tahoe. In 1853 mountain man John Calhoun "Cock-eye" Johnson and a reporter from the *Placerville Herald* followed the Rubicon River gorge into the lake basin and met a band of Washoes on the shore. The Indians communicated to them that they were the first white people to reach that spot, which later was named Meeks Bay. The Americans saw Cave Rock across the lake and asked about it. That night, so the story goes, a "wizened old [Washoe] patriarch 'poured forth from his shriveled lips the ancient legend of his tribe, concerning the rock and water prison of the Demons.'" Nowhere does the account explain how the Americans understood the Washoe language. The reporter's description of a trip across the lake in dugout canoes to the "mysterious grotto" further establishes the romantic nature of the account. The fantastic dimensions and features it portrays have little resemblance to the actual cave.

Other early Euro-American arrivals knew the site as "Rocky Point" and "Indian Rock." In 1855 pioneer surveyor George H. Goddard called Cave Rock the "legendary cave."[6]

After the discovery of the Comstock Lode in Virginia City, Nevada, in 1859, engineers built roads to facilitate traffic from San Francisco east across the Sierra Nevada to the gold and silver mines. The first roads emerged from the mountains in the south before reaching Cave Rock. In 1863 the construction of two roads north of the rock connected the Comstock to Lake Tahoe. The builders intended them to join with the southern highway to create the "Bonanza Road" (it was later called the Lincoln Highway and is today U.S. 50). Cave Rock stood as the main impediment to their plan. First, the road builders widened the deer trail behind the feature to accommodate wagons. When heavier freighters had difficulty pulling the grade, engineers constructed a trestle to support planking for a one-way bridge on the lake side of the rock, stacking rough quarried granite blocks to support the approaches to the wooden span. This segment, less than a mile long, cost $40,000, making it the most expensive piece of road in the Sierra Nevada. Although it was built below the cave, the bridge still stood some 75 feet above the lake. One observer wary of its precipitous vertical drop to the water noted that the jackstraw structure was "all that stood between the drivers of vehicles and eternity." The trestle foundation remains attached to Cave Rock today, a tribute to the ingenuity and abilities of nineteenth-century engineers.[7]

In 1931 a tunnel blasted through the rock replaced the plank bridge. A second round of blasting in 1957 created a second tunnel next to the first to accommodate increasing traffic. In neither instance did the road builders or the officials who authorized the roads consult the Washoes.[8]

Although Washoe religious practitioners continued to use the cave during these years, sightseers and partiers were far more conspicuous visitors. Some left behind debris or marked the cave with graffiti. Another type of visitor was about to become evident as well, adding to what the Washoes already perceived as a threat to their religion and their very way of life. Jay Smith built the first climbing route at Cave Rock. Smith's work eventually included four routes put up in April 1987 in the areas below the highway known as Lower Cave and Kona Wall.

For thirty years, enthusiasts had been free climbing the Sierra's rock walls with a minimum amount of hardware, much of it removable. Rappel bolting, or "rap bolting," in which a climber rappels from above in a harness to set bolts to hold belay ropes for sport climbers, had emerged at Tahoe in the mid-1980s. When sport rock climbers discovered Cave Rock, sometime around 1988, they began setting anchors in the granite to develop routes. Within several years the formation had become a world-renowned climbing site with the highest concentration of difficult sport climbs at Lake Tahoe. What Washoes regarded as a cultural shrine the *San Francisco Chronicle* described as "a [climbers'] refuge with the most gymnastic routes in the state."[9]

Sport climbers use athletic moves to master short, challenging routes rather than aiming for the easiest path to the top, valuing the "gain of inches in repeated attempts . . . above any straightforward push to a high summit."[10] The routes use permanent anchors to which climbers attach nylon slings that hold safety ropes. The large number of fixed features required in sport climbing caused controversy and antagonism in the Tahoe climbing community. Angry confrontations were accompanied by several cases of bolt chopping. Traditionalists argued that placing fixed anchors depleted the area's natural climbing resources. But the thrill of pursuing cutting-edge, extreme climbing won the war for the sport climbers. Climbing guidebook author Mike Carville reported that climbers finally decided they would "rather climb than whine," although "this does not imply that all of Tahoe's climbers embrace rap bolting." He counseled those seeking to set routes to "remain sensitive to the ethic of the area where they choose to climb."[11]

The sheer granite face at Cave Rock, which did not lend itself to traditional climbing, seemed to have been made for sport climbing. In 1989 Jay Smith and Paul Crawford, one of the region's leading ice climbers, put up routes on the rock face on both sides of the main cave. Over the next three years Smith, Crawford, and others—including Mike and Dave Hatchett, Dimitri Barton, Jason Campbell, and Dan Osman—created some twenty new lines. Carville noted that the face of Cave Rock began to resemble "a grid of bolts."[12]

In the early 1990s Osman used the site to hone skills that propelled him to extreme-sport superstar status while building several routes. The late Wolfgang Gullich, a German some consider the greatest sport climber in history, proclaimed one Osman route the "most elegant" he had ever climbed.[13]

The technical routes at Cave Rock, which included some of the highest rated in the nation, became the apex of the 112 climbing sites in the Lake Tahoe area. The complexities presented by the rock's overhang and steep walls, the quality of the routes, the ease of access to the site, and the aesthetic qualities of the setting contributed to its international reputation. The southwest face of the rock allowed year-round access, even during Tahoe's snowy winters. The Forest Service estimated that climber visits totaled between 1,100 and 1,500 annually.[14]

When Nevada officials proposed an expansion of the boat ramp below Cave Rock in 1992, the Washoe Tribal Council notified the state of the property's sacred status. While reviewing the boating project (which the tribe would fight against and lose) Brian Wallace, the newly elected Washoe tribal chair, became aware of the climbing apparatus in the rock and alerted the agency that would have ultimate jurisdiction, the U.S. Forest Service, to the damage being done by climbers. He responded to a Tahoe Regional Planning Agency query by saying, "We believe the most recent destruction of the Cave Rock site . . . adds insult to injury in the disturbing recent history of this very religious place." Wallace was renewing an old battle. The Washoe Tribal Council had petitioned to have the area designated as a landmark and memorial forty-one years earlier. In April 1951 the council voted six to zero "to publicly dedicate [a] roadside park at Cave Rock as a monument to the Indian people of the State of Nevada, and properly mark said park to point out the significance of its dedication." Although it attracted publicity in the form of articles in the local newspaper, the petition never gained approval, and within six years the state blasted the second tunnel through the rock.[15]

In April 1993 the *Tahoe Daily Tribune* quoted Wallace's claim that climbing and other recreational activities were desecrating "the most religious feature within the Washoe religion." In other interviews tribal elders expressed offense at the names of many of the routes, which included "Cave Man," "Super Monkey," "Trash Dog," "Bat Out of Hell," and "Shut the Fuck Up and Climb."[16]

Climbers reacted in various ways to the Washoes' concerns. Paul Crawford claimed that climbers had cleaned up "a rubble heap . . . left over from when tunnels were blasted through Cave Rock" and argued that "the tunnel itself took away any sacred value of the place." Dimitri Barton, whose route building included one constructed with Crawford, took the opposite view. Calling the site a "very, very special place" that he would hate to see off limits, he said he would stop climbing there to honor Washoe wishes, adding that the tribe had been "screwed enough" throughout history. Barton represented a minority of those interviewed. Most agreed with a Reno man who said, "We don't want to be an enemy to anybody. We just want to compromise and coexist. Everybody should have a chance to enjoy it." Brian Wallace worried that recent publicity would encourage further desecration, insisting that "a religious object of extreme significance is increasingly endangered." He announced that "officials of the Washoe Indian Tribe hope to ban rock climbing at Cave Rock."[17]

Startled by the Washoe leader's statements, several climbers contacted the Access Fund, a climbers' advocacy group founded in 1989, for help. Based in Boulder, Colorado, the organization works to keep climbing in public areas open and support climbers' constitutional rights. At the time, the group was already working to maintain climbing at Devil's Tower/Bear Lodge National Monument, a site in northeastern Wyoming sacred to Lakota, Cheyenne, and other Native communities. The Access Fund had joined forces with the seven commercial climbing guide companies at Devil's Tower/Bear Lodge to keep a closure requested by Indians for the ceremonial month of June voluntary rather than mandatory. The Access Fund's senior policy analyst summarized the group's objective: "If the climbing community chooses never to climb at some sacred sites out of respect for Native American beliefs, the Access Fund will support this position; if there is no broad-based agreement among climbers on such a gesture, we will work to ensure that those climbers who choose otherwise will not be penalized."[18]

The Access Fund brought ample resources to its challenge against the Washoe. More than seventy organizations were contributing financial support at that time, with some yearly corporate contributions exceeding $20,000.[19] In July 1993 the Access Fund's San Francisco–based attorney, Paul Minault, contacted the Tahoe Regional Planning Agency and the Forest Service in support of climbing at Cave Rock. When he asked to be included in any further meetings regarding its use, the battle loomed.[20]

The climbers maintained that they had the right to use the rock because it is on public land, and that a climbing prohibition would violate the multiple-use policy for federal lands. They also argued that the highway tunnels previously blown through the lower portion of the rock and the noise of the traffic using them had already irreparably damaged the site as a cultural property. The Washoe Tribal Council protested the scarring of the rock and the sustained human contact with it that climbing fostered. The council demanded that the activity stop and the anchors be removed.[21]

In 1996, because of its historical value and long association with the Washoe tribe, Cave Rock gained eligibility for inclusion on the National Register of Historic Places as a traditional cultural property. In February 1997 the U.S. Forest Service supervisor for Lake Tahoe imposed a temporary closure order forbidding climbing on the rock until the issue could be studied. After his retirement three months later, the new supervisor lifted the ban.

In 1998, two years after receiving the traditional cultural property designation, Cave Rock became eligible as a national historic transportation district while also being recognized for its archaeological importance. By then it hosted a steady stream of sport climbers from around the world. Part of the cave floor had been paved, and some 325 anchors marked forty-seven distinct technical routes on the rock face. At that time the Forest Service began attempts to mediate between the Washoe and the climbers. Their efforts failed, and the battle moved to the federal courts.[22]

This book chronicles the struggle between the Washoe tribe and the climbers who demanded the right to use Cave Rock for recreational purposes. The structure is at times more topical than chronological. The book commences with a brief overview of Washoe history, followed by the history of Euro-American activities at Cave Rock, in particular the roadway built around and through it. The narrative includes a treatment of shamanism, a tradition that has served the Washoe for thousands of years; a chapter about Henry Rupert, the Washoe healer most associated with the site; and a chapter on extreme sport star Dan Osman. It presents the philosophical positions of climbers who stopped using the site once it was identified as sacred, and those who insisted their rights would be violated if the Washoes prevailed. It tracks the strategies of the legal teams representing the two sides in the conflict and includes the travails of the Forest Service as its personnel attempted to find a just solution to the conundrum.

The account focuses on the rollercoaster history of events in the 1990s and early 2000s as the fate of the legendary landmark hung in the balance. In the end, the story of Cave Rock points to the fragile and halting nature of governmental decision making and the legal pitfalls and roadblocks Indian communities encounter as they work to protect culturally significant lands.

ONE

The Center

Native land bases have steadily disappeared since the first European colonists set foot in the Americas. Armed with an ethos that held Native people to be "savage" or at best "uncivilized," newcomers felt no compunction in appropriating their lands. By the time Euro-Americans arrived in Washoe country in the mid-1800s, a well-oiled colonial machine was systematically displacing Indian families. It did not help that Washoe territory contained some of the richest mineral bodies in North America. Ranchers, miners, and capitalists seeking their fortunes ignored Washoe claims to Sierra lands going back thousands of years.

Before Euro-Americans arrived the Washoe controlled a wide swath of the eastern Sierra. Villages occupied valleys, river basins, and, during the summer months, Lake Tahoe's shores. Communities engaged in cooperative ventures, celebrations, and mourning rites; they resolved territorial disputes through diplomacy and warfare. Specialists maintained and passed down vast knowledge of antelope and deer management, plant cultivation, fishing methods, food processing, and healing arts.

The California gold rush and the subsequent discovery of the Comstock Lode in Nevada in the mid-nineteenth century brought thousands of foreigners into Washoe lands. Newcomers viewed the sweeping valleys, rugged mountains, and numerous waterways as an empty Eden whose minerals, timber, grasslands, plants, animals, and fish were free for the taking. By the time federal officials got involved, the best properties had been privatized, deforested, and depleted. The Washoes had become strangers in their own land.

The dominating American presence rapidly eclipsed a tenuous peace long held by the Washoes with their neighbors, the Northern Paiute, Western Shoshone, Maidu, and Miwok peoples. Age-old diplomatic and defense strategies no longer availed the small Sierra community.

Daowaga (Lake Tahoe) was the keystone for Washoe cultural identity. In 1961 Tribal Chair Earl James explained that twentieth-century Washoes had learned from their ancestors, who had learned "from their forefathers," that Tahoe was the center—the heart—of their lands. For countless generations Cave Rock had loomed above this center, its use restricted to the most powerful shamans.[1]

Today most Washoes speak about Cave Rock with reserve. Darrel Bender, a tribal elder and nephew of the late shaman Dick Bagley, noted that "Indian doctors didn't explain to us what they did up there but it was something to do with power" and involved extremely "secretive and sacred rites."[2]

The last doctor seen using Cave Rock was Mike Dick (sometimes called "Blind Mike"). Accompanied by his wife, Dick stood on a rock in the water near the cave and attempted to use a secret, underwater entrance. He began reciting a song given to him through dreams, and the rock started to sink. His wife screamed at the sight, disrupting the incantation, and Dick was left standing knee-deep in the water.[3]

Archaeological evidence corroborates the oral tradition that claims ancestral Washoes did not use the cave as a shelter or homesite. Had it been one, archaeologists would have found evidence of human habitation in the form of tools and debris. The items recovered there, including the oldest artifacts—an inscribed mammal bone and three basalt projectile points—imply a more esoteric use.[4]

For thousands of years Lake Tahoe drew Washoe families together during the spring and summer months. Members of distinct, far-flung communities traveled to the lake's shores from their winter homes in the eastern Sierra foothills and valleys. The Welmelti, or northern Washoes, inhabited the valleys and foothills around what is today Reno, Nevada, and Susanville, California. The Pawaltis, or valley-dwellers, lived just east of Lake Tahoe in the present-day Carson and Eagle valleys. To the south lived the Hangalelti, or southerners, whose traditional territory ranged as far south as Sonora Pass, California.

The western reaches of the Sierra provided a fluid boundary, its exact location dependent on encroachments or retreats by Washoes and neighboring California communities. The range of the piñon pine, bordering Nevada's Great Basin, delineated an eastern border. The Washoes depended on the piñons' nutritious fruits, or pine nuts, to get them through the winter. Communities took advantage of the eastern Sierra's ecological diversity and tailored their lives to an annual seasonal cycle.

Spring announced the beginning of the "big time," the gathering of the people at Lake Tahoe. The young and healthy were the first to set out from their valley homes. A trek that today takes perhaps thirty minutes to an hour by car, depending on the point of origin, would have taken a day or more on foot. The older and less healthy ones who followed took longer, camping along the way at familiar spots. Once settled at the lake, tribal members would visit relatives, share news and gossip, hold ceremonies, take advantage of the spring fish runs, and prepare for summer harvests.

During the late stages of summer, families spread out, visiting the trading grounds in the western Sierra foothills. Here, in times of peace, Washoes exchanged news and resources with neighboring Maidu and Miwok communities. By fall most Washoes had worked their way back to the valleys east of the Sierra.

Autumn provided the setting for the dagoomsabye, or pine nut festival, which was held in the Tah gum a shia (Pine Nut Hills). Families gathered for days of prayers, games, visits, feasts, and harvesting. Afterward they returned to their valley homes to prepare for winter. Foods had to be processed and stored, living quarters had to be insulated, and hunters worked to stock the food cache. By the first freeze, if all went as planned, Washoe families were ready to spend the winter engaged in handicrafts, tool and weapon making, storytelling, and short hunting treks as they awaited the signs of spring that would signal a return to their center, Daowaga.

Across their diverse homelands Washoe families maintained ma-ash (family property), which might include creeks, streams, springs, pine stands, sage lands, and piñon groves. Ma-ash lands also crossed spiritually significant and medicinal lands; and there were the places of power—none more important than Cave Rock. Doctors used the cave to connect with powerful forces. Darrel Bender commented, "It is hard to explain what [Washoe doctors] did because it was a very, very personal thing." When Bender asked his uncle, Dick Bagley, or elders about Cave Rock, the usual response was: "It is none of your business." Metaphysical forces would let a person know whether to pursue power, which held danger, perhaps including death, for those who used it.[5]

Bender helped his uncle prepare for the trip to Cave Rock twice a year. He estimated that Bagley's work at Cave Rock, including preparations, took up to one month. It took him "three or four days to get to the actual spot at Cave Rock because there were different rites or ceremonies and prayers" to perform along the way. What Bagley did at Cave Rock remains unknown; Bender knows only that he worked there for a "renewal of power." The land's new Euro-American inhabitants, who brought far-reaching changes, strained Bagley's use of Cave Rock, as well as that of other practitioners.[6]

Foreign nations did not encroach on Washoe lands with intentions to stay until the official surveying expedition of John Charles Frémont arrived in 1844. The Washoes Frémont encountered gave him handfuls of pine nuts, a traditional welcome, and one young Washoe acted as a guide. Four years later, the United States signed the Treaty of Guadalupe Hidalgo formally ending a war with Mexico, which ceded California and Nevada, among other western lands, to the United States. Washoe country now fell within U.S. territory.

The discovery of gold near Sutter's Mill in 1848 brought frenetic urgency to American expansion. Eleven years later the immense veins of Comstock Lode silver in Virginia City, Nevada, brought a second migratory wave. By the 1860s, territorial and federal officials had noted a by-product of American colonization: Washoe destruction.

An agent for the federal government, Jacob Lockhart, observed in 1862: "The wild game is being killed by the whites, the trees from which the Indians gathered nuts are being cut down, and the grass from which they gathered seeds for winter is being taken from them." Lockhart went on to request two federal land reserves (reservations) of 360 acres each for the Washoe people.[7] Federal officials failed to act on the suggestion.

The government official who succeeded Lockhart viewed the problem from a different perspective. The new superintendent of Nevada Indian affairs, Hubbard G. Parker, deemed Lockhart's request for reservations "unadvisable and inexpedient." The following year Parker offered a glimpse into the Washoe world of the 1860s: "A few have learned the English language, and will do light work for a reasonable compensation. They spend the winter months about the villages and habitations of white men, from whom they obtain tolerable supplies of food and clothing. The spring, summer and autumn months are spent in fishing about Washoe and Tahoe lakes and the streams which flow through their country. They also gather grass-seed and pine-nuts, hunt rabbits, hares, and ducks."[8]

Parker's report indicates that the Washoes, limited in land use and resources, continued to move with the seasons in a precarious balance between traditions and a changing world. Parker concluded with a disturbingly callous observation that, due to their "rapidly diminishing numbers," the Washoes did not need a reservation.[9]

Thirty years after Parker's pronouncement, however, the Washoes had not disappeared. To the contrary, they had begun to use legal and bureaucratic channels to regain pieces of their land. In 1893, for example, Washoes used the Dawes Act to reacquire 87,000 acres of their ancestral pine-nut lands. Federal officials had tailored the Dawes Act (commonly called the Allotment Act) to accelerate Indian assimilation by carving tribal lands into small, individual allotments. The creation of Indian boarding schools in the late 1880s was another federal strategy to "kill the Indian but save the man."[10]

Section 4 of the Dawes Act stated that landless tribes could use the act to gain acreage. The act was partially intended to make Indians into American farmers. But under the leadership of Gumalanga, known as "Captain Jim," a Washoe delegation successfully lobbied for and acquired the non-irrigable but culturally important pine-nut lands.[11]

By 1916 federal agents had recognized two things: first, owning pine-nut lands would not turn Washoes into American farmers; and, second, the pine-nut allotments would not sustain Washoe families. That same year, after frustrating dogged lobbying by impoverished Washoe individuals, including Captain Jim, the federal government finally appropriated $10,000 to purchase lands for Washoe use. To oversee the appropriation the government sent Agent Lorenzo Creel, who hired a Washoe interpreter, Ben James, and set out to visit the various Washoe camps across the Carson Valley and southern Eagle Valley. Creel's census counted close to two hundred Washoe families living on or near ranches, where they worked as ranch hands and domestic servants. Creel informed officials in Washington, D.C., that many Washoes did not want to meet him or talk with him because they believed the federal government might be setting a trap.

Armed with census statistics and a firsthand view of Washoe living conditions, Creel lobbied earnestly for good irrigable lands. But local ranchers and landowners made Creel's work difficult. Washoes had become their primary labor force, and they worried that if Washoe families acquired their own land they might be unwilling to work for others. Consequently, the landowners refused to sell. Finally, Carson Valley rancher Fred Dressler agreed to give up forty acres adjacent to the Carson River, albeit without water rights. Even without the rights, the land was an improvement over temporary camps on the fringes of white-owned ranches. Creel went on to secure additional plots of land in Reno and on the outskirts of Carson City. Washoe families set to work building new communities, whose center remains today at the original property called Dresslerville.[12]

From their new homesites many Washoes carved out a place within American society. They continued to work as ranch hands and domestic servants, and with great ingenuity managed to sustain a form of their traditional seasonal cycle. Although by the twentieth century Lake Tahoe had been largely privatized, Washoe individuals continued to spend the summer months there, now working for the tourist resorts. Men cut wood and performed maintenance duties while women worked as laundresses and cooks.

Elder Belma Jones remembered her grandfather taking the seat out of his wagon to make a flatbed, which he loaded with bedding and children to make the trip to Tahoe in the early twentieth century. Everybody else hiked up the steep, windy mountainside. "There was a trail, this is the old Kingsbury road," Jones recalled. "Man, that was some road. . . . There were a lot of Indians who went up there." Jones and her generation encountered a Tahoe much different from the one their ancestors knew. Instead of access to all the lake's resources, Washoes in the twentieth century found barbed wire, clear-cuts, and tourist resorts. "People began to fence their land and then it all became private," Jones said, "because we used to swim anywhere and there weren't any houses, you know, on the beach like now. We used to go from the north shore clear over to what is now that estate there [Valhalla on the south shore] and there was a place called Camp Richardson. . . . Later people began to fence, so we couldn't go through there anymore." Meanwhile, Washoe doctors, including the young Henry Rupert, an apprentice of the acclaimed shaman Beleliwe, continued making their periodic visits to Cave Rock.[13]

Many Washoe community members supplemented their income by adapting traditional practices such as fishing and basket weaving to the

American market. Some Washoe fishermen sold their catch to resorts; others acted as guides for vacationing sportsmen. Women began shaping their formerly utilitarian willow baskets to fit the growing tourist market and quickly earned respect for their artistic design and mastery.

A Washoe woman born around 1835 named Datsolalee became the most famous of all western Indian basket weavers in the nineteenth century. By the last quarter of the century even her smallest products sold for an amazing fifty dollars apiece. By the early 1900s these same baskets could not "be purchased for ten times that sum." Simeon Lemuel Lee, M.D., a Civil War veteran who collected baskets from across the West, called her masterpiece "Migration" "one of the finest Indian baskets in the world." The 8-inch-by-12-inch piece, with a 35-inch circumference and 6-inch opening, contained more than 50,000 stitches—30 per inch. Dr. Lee's detailed inventory of the pieces he acquired reveals the genius of Washoe weavers and their growing ability to craft their wares for an American market. A basket he called "the gem of the Washoes," made by Datsolalee's cousin Ceese, was equally magnificent. He explained that Ceese was to Datsolalee "what Rafael was to Michael Angelo. She may not be superior . . . but in no way is she inferior." Lee paid Abe Cohen, a collector and patron of Datsolalee, five twenty-dollar gold pieces for Ceese's "gem." Lee did not indicate how much of the hundred dollars made it to Ceese. While Datsolalee's agent sold her wares, less-well-known weavers marketed their own works in the summers, often on the shores of Lake Tahoe.[14]

Even into the late twentieth century Washoes continued their fall trips to the pine-nut lands. Washoe Bernice Auchoberry, born in 1914, explained: "We always went out every fall, every September, and we'd go out and gather nuts. We'd get enough for the winter." The grandson of ranch owner Fred Dressler recalled that ranchers became accustomed to the seasonal activities of their hired hands. "Indian folks were never a year-round employee; they were periodic," Dressler said. "When they were hungry, they went fishing or hunting and they supplied their wants and quit. They always had to take time off."[15]

Even with a semblance of their seasonal cycle intact, the Washoes suffered terribly during the early twentieth century. Destitution and disease plagued them. In 1936 the Washoe incorporated under the U.S. Indian Reorganization Act, writing a constitution and setting up a tribal government to mirror the American federal government. Now "officially" recognized, Washoes began working to protect their communities. But the subsequent decades brought perpetual difficulties.

During the 1940s the Washoe Tribal Council initiated a lawsuit against the federal government for lands wrongfully taken. From the beginning of the legal proceedings the federal government made it clear that the Washoes could not sue to regain lands, only for monetary compensation. The case stretched into the late 1960s, requiring a large amount of the council's time and resources. At the conclusion of the case the federal government awarded the Washoes a disappointing five million dollars. The sum was intended as recompense for all lands at Lake Tahoe and Carson City, and 1.5 million acres of prime mining, residential, and ranch lands. A healthy portion of the award went to legal fees.

In 1970 the Washoes used an appropriation from Congress to establish the Woodfords colony consisting of eighty acres on a rocky shelf in Alpine County, California. A 1973 grant from the U.S. Department of Commerce Economic Development Administration enabled the council to build a public campground on the Carson River.[16]

The tribe created the Washoe Cultural Foundation in the early 1980s to work to secure land at Lake Tahoe. The Washoe tribe won a competitive bid for a twenty-year lease in 1988 to act as proprietor of the popular Lake Tahoe resort at Meeks Bay. Meadows behind the resort are being utilized to harvest traditional medicinal and food plants.

In the early 1990s, having regained use of a piece of their traditional center, the Washoes turned their attention to Cave Rock. A government that had overseen the destruction of their homeland, failed to allocate them reservation land, and allotted scant compensation for their losses would now be charged with determining justice regarding their claim at Cave Rock.

TWO

The Tunnels

The two highway tunnels that penetrate the granite below the main, or upper, cave at Cave Rock played an important part in the dispute regarding climbing and Washoe spirituality at the site. Early in the controversy, portions of the area were closed to climbing because of the danger of rockfall onto the roadway below. While accepting that limited closure, climbers argued that most of the area should remain open, claiming that the site was no longer sacred or meaningful to the Washoes because of the tunnels' traffic and noise. Ironically, in the final decision the tunnels would weigh against the climbers. The tunnels figured significantly in the 1998 finding that Cave Rock qualified as a national historic transportation district. The new status added another element to Cave Rock's consideration for eligibility to the National Register.

Early-twentieth-century bureaucrats and planners gave little thought to the imposition of machine technology on culture. In 1928, however, University of Chicago sociologist William F. Ogburn published an article on inventions in the *American Journal of Sociology*. He acknowledged the strangeness of writing about mechanical devices in a periodical dealing with social change, but argued that it was not only acceptable but obligatory. He observed that mechanical changes positively or negatively affected the social welfare of human beings. "Indeed," he wrote, "it may be argued, with some success that the origins of most of the innumerable social changes occurring today lie in new inventions of a mechanical nature."[1] Events in early-twentieth-century Nevada supported his thesis, in particular with regard to the automobile and its effects on numerous aspects of life; it certainly proved true for the Washoes and Cave Rock.

At the beginning of the twentieth century the automobile industry and the railroads were battling for the loyalty of the American traveler. In 1900 the old Madison Square Garden hosted the nation's first auto show.

By 1903 a magazine named *Outing* touted the possibility of rediscovering America by automobile. Local chambers of commerce and enterprises that would profit from car traffic—car makers and sellers; the rubber, oil, cement, and road machinery industries; and quarry, sand, and gravel pit businesses—promoted automobile travel. In the 1920s the automobile industry won the battle and the car became America's preeminent mode of travel. But unlike the railroad, the auto industry had developed its rolling stock well before sufficient roadways were present to carry it.[2]

Advocates of the automobile initially promoted local road building. The federal government created the Office of Public Roads in 1905, but the agency served essentially as an advisory body and provided few funds. In 1912 Congress approved funds for building roads in the national forests and parks, but it was not until 1916, stimulated by the idea of a national, coast-to-coast highway, that the government established substantial assistance for a road system. A group of cars that worked its way over local roads on a proposed central overland route from the Midwest to San Francisco generated publicity for the idea. When its promoters attached the name "Lincoln" to the proposed national highway, the idea captured America's fancy. In fall 1913 the Lincoln Highway Association began organizing national propagandizing, and in July 1916 the federal government became actively involved, passing the Federal Highway Aid Act.[3]

Money from federal, state, and county coffers funded the suddenly rapid development of roads and highways. Ohio, for example, spent $460 on its roads in 1905 and $17 million in 1926. Along with passenger and commercial utilization, medical, school, and mail services made extensive use of the roads.[4] In 1927, after eight years of work, the incredible 9,250-foot-long Holland Tunnel beneath the Hudson River was completed. Meanwhile, engineers in the West designed the greatest structure of the generation—the Golden Gate Bridge—although it would not be completed until 1937.

In mid-January 1931 the Forest Service highway funds program allotted $245,833 to the state of Nevada. Of that amount planners designated $86,000 for construction of three miles of the Lincoln Highway from Cave Rock to Zephyr Cove. Most of that money was to be used to bore a 151-foot tunnel through Cave Rock for a two-lane highway. A portion of the funds would create a parking and viewing area west of the old trestle road. The Nevada Department of Highways predicted that "the completion of this thoroughly modern and beautifully scenic highway along the rim of Lake Tahoe will increase tourist travel to Lake Tahoe and adjacent points in Nevada to a marked extent."[5]

In early May the Nevada Highway Office in Carson City announced that it would accept bids for the tunnel beginning on May 29. The announcement specified a standard twenty-four-foot road and said that "the big rock must not be injured in any manner," although one report stated that galleries were to be cut through the face of the rock at intervals "in order to give tourists a view of Lake Tahoe." Plans also included steps built up to the main cave above the road, but neither the galleries nor the steps were ever constructed.[6]

No one consulted—or even notified—the Washoe tribe regarding the proposed tunnel. The tribe was still fragmented at that point and lacked a recognized government. In any case, the whites, as a rule, did not talk to the Washoes. In Minden, for example, just outside the Lake Tahoe basin, Indians worked for whites, but those found within the town limits when the evening siren sounded were subject to arrest.[7]

Two local newspaper articles published in April 1931 reflect the Washoes' plight. The first notes the desire of Hank Pete, the grandson of Captain Pete—one of the Washoes' leaders when the first Euro-Americans arrived in Nevada—to meet with a committee on Indian affairs scheduled to visit the state in the near future. He wanted to point out how unfairly the government had treated the Washoes and to petition the committee for federal assistance. Pete pointed out the irony of the Washoes' predicament. While other Nevada tribes had warred against the influx of colonists, the Washoes had been peaceful—and had in fact offered to help the government check the warlike tribes' depredations. The tribes that fought the United States had then gained federal recognition while the Washoes had been placed on forty acres of land without water rights.[8]

An article a week later reported that the Indian children of Nevada were soon to be allowed a benefit heretofore denied them: they could attend public schools up to the eighth grade. The movement was part of the Department of the Interior's program of integration aimed at "breaking up the isolated radical groups on the reservations, and getting their members to work among the general population." The Washoe children would soon gain the benefit of an "up-to-date" education and the experience of having contact with "American normal life." As implied by Hank Pete's concerns, contact with American life for the children did not lead to similar consideration of Washoe concerns regarding the boring of a roadway at Lake Tahoe.[9]

The Nevada Construction Company won the contract for the Cave Rock tunnel and brought Stanley Bray in to engineer the project. Bray had considerable experience, having supervised the creation of the new 1.1-mile tunnel on the Mount Zion highway in Bryce Canyon, Utah—one of the longest and most expensive road construction projects ever attempted in the United States.

The company hired workers and built a camp for them near the lake. When two men seeking employment raised questions about the camp's sanitation, an inspector for the Nevada health office came out to investigate. Although his report presented a few recommendations for improvement, the inspector adjudged the camp one of the best in the state and labeled its sanitation "splendid."

During the tunnel's construction the company closed the hanging bridge above the lake, forcing traffic to use the old trail behind Cave Rock. Many travelers criticized the detour's poor condition, but their complaints went unheeded; Bray's men were focused on the job at hand. They swung heavy cables down over the rock face in preparation for the drilling, and by June 26 had moved their machinery and materials into place. The work would continue into October, although cars began to be allowed to pass through the tunnel in mid-September. The order of the day was "drill, load, tamp, set the charge and then run like hell." Washoes in Carson Valley later recounted feeling the shocks when the blasts occurred.[10]

The Washoes felt similar shocks twenty-six years later in 1957 when a second tunnel was blasted into the rock. Newly developed ski resorts and neon-lit casinos at Lake Tahoe encouraged year-round tourism, and the tunnel had created a bottleneck on the lake's south shore. Policy planners determined that a second tunnel through Cave Rock was needed to carry the extra traffic. Although the Washoes had their own tribal government by this time, they had no access to the land use agencies that made such decisions, and no one consulted them. Another twenty-five years would pass before Congress or the courts afforded tribes the opportunity to participate in decisions regarding traditional properties.[11]

Bidding for the second excavation began on October 11, 1956. The existing tunnel was 153 feet long; the new one, closer to the main cave's face, was to be 410 feet long. In preparation for the project, the U.S. Bureau of Public Roads had financed the removal of thousands of cubic yards of earth on the approaches to the new bore. This material had been used to construct a roadway down to the lake where a roadside park and boat ramp were being built. The local newspaper predicted that the adjunct project would be "one of Douglas County's prime attractions for tourists, meeting a long-recognized need for additional free public recreational facilities on the lakeshore."[12]

A firm based in Salt Lake City, Utah, won the bid for construction of the second tunnel. The $455,717 cost would be split between the state of Nevada and the federal government. By December, workers had attacked the rock from the north and south while dump trucks hauled the blasted-out material down to the roadside park. Nevada Department of Highways press releases identified Cave Rock as "one of the best known landmarks at Lake Tahoe." Articles in the local paper made a point of referring to the site as "historic," "famed," and "the scenic attraction." None of the publicity mentioned the Washoe legacy at Cave Rock.

Use of explosives was more precise in the 1950s than in 1931. Each shot, produced by drilling 150 holes to distribute 450 pounds of dynamite, blasted eight feet out of the rock. After each detonation, fired alternately in the north and south bores, workers removed the debris and set timbers for the next shot.[13]

Traditional Washoes believe that those who misuse Cave Rock put themselves, and perhaps others, in jeopardy. And indeed, accidents plagued the project. A two-and-a-half-yard power shovel fell over a steep embankment. A few weeks later, a foreman working on the mountain side of the highway near the work site slammed the door of his parked pickup truck and accidentally released the emergency brake. The truck began to move, gaining momentum as it went. It crossed the road and catapulted over the nearly perpendicular embankment. The pickup rolled at least three times on the way down and, flattened, plunged into the lake. Only a small part of the truck's bed was visible from above.

Several weeks after that incident a worker's leg was crushed when, without warning, a five-hundred-pound rock careened down the monolith's granite face. The multiple compound fractures he sustained necessitated amputation.

Superintendents proved difficult to keep on the project, and three were employed over the course of the construction. The original proposal called for completion of the job by June 1, well in advance of the heavy summer travel. The ongoing problems forced officials repeatedly to postpone the opening: to June 15, July 15, August 5, and finally August 16, when the project was completed.[14]

Once again the Washoes could only watch as progress brought further disorder to their world.

THREE

Real Powers

In Carson City, Nevada, on a hot summer day in the 1880s, Dr. Simeon Lee treated an elderly Washoe man who had fallen face-down in a dusty street. Lee ruled the collapse a result of heat exhaustion. On his follow-up visit the next day, Lee found the man sitting between two women who were chanting rhythmically. Also in attendance was a boy Lee described as a "bright faced young full blooded Washoe lad of, perhaps 19." The boy offered his own diagnosis for the collapse: witchcraft. He explained that "an enemy at Double Springs had blown poison into the sufferer although they were separated by twenty long miles." When Dr. Lee asked who the victim was, the young man replied: "He is captain of all the Double Springs Washoe, all Carson Valley Washoes, all the Markleeville Washoes, all the Reno Washoes, Captain Jimmie." In the Washoe world, even the most influential were susceptible to a witch's power.[1]

The difference between Lee's diagnosis and the boy's exposes the gulf separating the Washoe world from mainstream America in the nineteenth century. This distance gradually narrowed as American cultural impositions altered the Washoes' healing traditions and worldview. A Washoe individual interviewed in the 1950s noted the almost complete disappearance of Washoe shamans. He believed that diseases could be cured effectively with American medicine and Washoes no longer needed the "real powers" formerly cultivated and used by shamans.[2]

In the pre-American Washoe world, wegeléyu (power) permeated the universe. This autonomous force existed independently from living beings. Neither good nor bad, wegeléyu's essence animated the living world. A select few Washoes, the dreamers and shamans, developed extraordinary skills when they tapped into wegeléyu's constant flow.[3]

A clear distinction separated "curers" from shamans. Generally, Washoe women knew herbs and plants intimately and could prescribe cures for common ailments. Shamans, those who healed and those who used power for other purposes, could be male or female. They exercised power on a different level.[4]

Power could not be gained through vision quests or solitary pilgrimages. It came of its own accord, usually through dreams. The content of power dreams varied, but generally they included significant figures such as bears, eagles, deer, rattlesnakes, water beings, or apparitions. One shaman's son, speaking in the 1950s, said that the dream could "take any form, a skeleton or an animal but you know it's always the same thing . . . just taking different shapes." George Snooks, son of Tom Snooks (who trained to become a shaman), said that power dreams adopted different shapes but emphasized that the dream "must have life." Tom Snooks' mentor, Mike Dick, considered power dreams that included animals or water beings to be "most important." Dick explained unequivocally that power chose the person, not the other way around. "It depends on the spirit. If the spirit wants to help, you become a shaman." The best-known Washoe shaman of the twentieth century, Henry Rupert, echoed Dick's assertion that the dreamer has no choice in the matter, "The dream has to come to him—even though he wants it bad." More recently Darrel Bender explained that power "comes to you, then you train. It is not something where you say, 'Oh, I am going to be an Indian doctor or a medicine man,' and start training. Washoe way is not that way—it comes to you."[5]

Dreams also offered songs and procedural practices to potential doctors. Henry Rupert's dreams taught him ancient songs of the loon and bear that he used in healing rites. Tom Snooks followed the instructions given in dreams. Eventually he received four or five songs, roughly one per year.[6]

The role of dreams in the acquisition of power is not solely a Washoe phenomenon. From the aboriginal dream time of Australia to the dreaming doctors of California, dreams have served Native communities around the world. The last of the Cache Creek Losel Pomo medicine people in California, Mabel Mckay, relied on dreams for curing and for her weaving designs. Mckay claimed that all guidance came from the spirit, which visited her in dreams. When asked her age when her dreams started, Mckay responded, "It didn't have no start. It goes on." With regard to her weaving Mabel said that the spirit showed her "everything. Each basket has a Dream."[7]

Yuman-speaking Indians along the Colorado River believed in sumach ahot (great dreams) and held that children dreamed before birth. Doctors among their southern neighbors, the Quechan, also put great stock in prebirth and childhood dreams. A Quechan storyteller recounted his prenatal dreams to the well-known California anthropologist Alfred Kroeber. The man told Kroeber that although he would steal out of his mother's womb while she was sleeping, he would not go far. Later, as a boy, his dreams took him all the way to the sacred Avi Kwame Mountain, where he met Kumastambo, the Creator.[8]

Among the Washoe, those who dreamed gained access to power, and power often stayed within doctoring families. One elder noted, "Them people that [are] from a doctor family, they have dreams and get curing power." Another individual expressed the inevitability of the family link: "If you come from a family of dreamers there ain't nothing you can do. You're trapped by it."[9]

The best course for an individual visited by power was to work with an experienced shaman. "Although doctors develop themselves naturally," Rupert explained, "older doctors boost along younger ones giving advice and direction." Established doctors could help the neophytes either develop their power or get rid of it. Either way, something had to be done. Power ignored could be life threatening or might manifest itself in other unhealthy ways. Mike Dick taught dreamers to "do everything exactly as he is told in the dream. There must be no slips." Dreams often directed the individual to perform a difficult task. Dick assured his pupils that those who did not follow their dream's instructions would "get sick and die every time."[10]

One of the most respected doctors in the early twentieth century, Beleliwe, told students, "You can't get rid of [power] unless you die." Doctors watched their potential pupils carefully. Any indication that the training was not going as it should might prompt the mentor to "kill the power."[11]

The process of becoming a doctor was personalized by the nature and extent of the initiate's power source, but a general training protocol did exist. Edgar Siskin, an anthropologist who worked with a number of Washoe shamans in the late 1930s, described a thirty-two-day cycle of training broken up into four-day intervals. This cycle could be used several times during a dreamer's training.

Siskin documented the process of obtaining a moth cocoon rattle, a tool many Washoe doctors used for healing rites. If the dream instructed a novice to get a rattle, the individual acted in specific ways for thirty-two days. Fasting occupied the first four days. Rupert described fasting as "the main thing," indicating that meat, salt, and onions had to be avoided. Hank Pete, whose mother was a shaman, remembered his mother not eating meat and avoiding grease or salt.[12]

The gathering of necessary items took place in the four-day interval after fasting, followed by a four-day period of rest and then four days of making the rattle. The next cycle included four days of dedication—praying over the rattle—alternating with four days of doing nothing. On the last day of the cycle the dreamer sprinkled water on the completed rattle.

Potential doctors went through cycles similar to this for an unspecified number of years. According to Rupert, one person might complete the training in four years while another might take sixteen. He concluded, "Anyway it is a lifetime of study." In his estimation doctors did not begin healing until they had reached their forties.[13]

Some dreamers worked hard for many years without ever completing their training. Tom Snooks, for example, began by following his dream. During the initial training period the experienced shaman Mike Dick came to live with him. Snooks began to heal people, but only in the presence of his mentor. At some point, Snooks and Dick parted ways. Snooks died shortly thereafter. Some claimed Snooks unwittingly contracted an illness he had extracted from a patient; others believed he had been ensorcelled by a Washoe witch. In either view the hazards of shamanic training were manifest.[14]

The anthropologist who has done the most work with the Washoes, Warren d'Azevedo, described a "profound ambivalence" among Washoes regarding shamans. Doctors' relationship with power and access to secrets "inaccessible to other persons" exempted them from the constraints of normal social behavior. This was not something to be taken lightly. Washoe history is replete with tales of sorcery. An individual wielding power with malice could kill telepathically. More common was an evil doctor, often called a witch (a term applied to both men and women), causing "illness and misfortune" to an enemy.[15]

George Snooks claimed that "a doctor who doesn't like you can shoot his power at you when you are passing by." Powerful doctors could extend their reach across vast distances. Susie Rube recounted the work of an evil doctor named Detutudi from the southern Washoe lands. Detutudi once made a trip to Walley's Hot Springs, near present-day Genoa, Nevada, in central Washoe country. The valley dwellers did not like him, and let him know it. Before he left, Detutudi warned a woman who had fed him that he was going home to concoct a killing spell but intended to spare her and her daughter. Within the week Detutudi cast his power, from thirty miles away, to the hot springs. In its wake the power left dead trees, grasses, and weeds. When it hit the hot springs, everyone died except the woman and her daughter. A trail of destruction scarred the land between the two sites.[16]

All Washoe doctors had the ability to use power maliciously, but not all did so. Henry Rupert shunned the dark arts and worked to heal, not harm. He used water as his primary power source, and that required him to develop a relationship with water beings.

Over the past fifty years anthropologists working with Washoes have written widely about small, mysterious beings with transcendent power said to inhabit streams, rivers, springs, and lakes across the Sierra. A popular Washoe story tells of a non-Washoe fisherman who accidentally captured one of these odd-looking beings and donated it to an aquarium in San Francisco, California. The being eventually broke free—in the process causing the great earthquake of 1906.[17]

The waters of Lake Tahoe around Cave Rock formed the hub of the water beings' world. Cave Rock itself provided a portal for them to travel throughout Washoe lands. This aspect of the Washoe mythological narrative at least partly explains the site's importance to doctors who communicated with, and drew power from, the water beings.

Native Americans recognized power places all across the American West. In a legal brief for an Indian claims case during the 1950s, Alfred Kroeber cited "literally tens of thousands of such natural features or spots throughout California having magical or religious or legendary meaning and significance." More recently Peter Nabokov explained: "The spirits of their [Natives'] stories inhabited mountains, knolls, oddly shaped rocks, coastal overlooks, river whirlpools, slit caves and seepage holes."[18]

Reconceived by successive waves of human inhabitants, these sites have not lost their significance. The Hopis' reverence for shrine sites within their mesas preceded the wholly geographical perspective of the Spanish, which preceded the similarly secular viewpoints of the Mexicans and Americans. Hopis did not abandon their view because of the impositions of the others.

The well-being of sacred areas such as the Hopi shrines and Cave Rock has been the concern of Native peoples for thousands of years. Some believe that their very survival depends on them, just as Washoes believe the misuse of Cave Rock is a threat to individuals and communities alike.[19]

The late Vine Deloria Jr. tried to explain a worldview in which land, especially sacred land, requires something from its human occupants. Humans, he wrote, must consider ceremonial functions "required . . . to remain worthy of living there."[20] In the case of Cave Rock, Washoes feel the necessity to reserve its use exclusively for shamanistic rites.

Washoe individuals find it difficult to describe the transcendent importance of Cave Rock. When it comes to shared use with climbers, no compromise is possible. Cave Rock is meant to be accessible only to those who can manage its power. Brian Wallace explained, "Traditionally there are just certain types of Washoe people that have the authority, the power, the teaching, and background to become a part of Cave Rock, [to] know the power of the site." Likewise, Lisa Grayshield noted: "To actually go to Cave Rock . . . is not something that we are taught to do. . . . That's a sacred site for our medicine people." She wished non-Washoes to understand that tribal members wanted the site closed to honor the "elders [who] take care of that [place] for us." Viewed in this light, the Cave Rock dispute cannot be dismissed as Indian people wanting to keep other Americans out of traditional lands for baseless, punitive, or arbitrary reasons. For modern-day Washoes to pay homage to ancestors, shamans, and elders while simultaneously honoring the needs of Cave Rock and the land itself, they cannot compromise.[21]

FOUR

The Innovator

The fame and influence of Henry Rupert, the shaman most often publicly associated with Cave Rock, cross cultural boundaries. He is the only Washoe doctor to be the subject of a published ethnology. The resonance of his healing abilities became a primary consideration when the Forest Service was making a final determination at Cave Rock.[1]

When Rupert was a young man, a dream revealed that water would be his primary source of power. Only Washoe doctors who had a relationship with water and water beings could use Cave Rock. The intrusion of Euro-American sightseers and fishermen at the site, later compounded by automobile traffic passing through the tunnels, altered what had once been a solitary activity. Rupert adapted to these changes and continued to use the cave throughout his lifetime, although he never publicly discussed his association with it. Anthropologist James Downs, who visited Rupert in the late 1950s, claimed that Rupert "did not deny his shamanistic practices but was less than willing to discuss them in detail." Rupert spoke little of his healing prowess in general, explaining: "I am not allowed to brag about my work and tell people what I can do." He said he did not use his power for "money-making or riches"; he used it exclusively "for helping people." He concluded, "You don't advertise this kind of work."[2]

Rupert's reluctance to divulge elements of his healing practices has not obscured his role as an innovator. He developed a cosmology and healing methods grounded in both Washoe and Western traditions, building a cultural bridge between his own indigenous healing practices and the Euro-American world. During his lifetime Rupert's power as a curer spread beyond the small Washoe communities of the eastern Sierra, and he healed a substantial number of non-Native patients. People across the Sierra sought Rupert out when physicians or other healers had failed. The farmers, businesspeople, and even a white Protestant minister whom he restored to health affirmed the efficacy of Rupert's power.

Rupert grew up with his mother, Susie John, in a small Washoe community. His father, Pete Duncan, left the family when Rupert was two or three years old. Susie John worked as a domestic servant for a non-Washoe family in Genoa, Nevada, the state's first non-Native town. Because of its year-round water supply, hot springs, and rich hunting grounds, this area of the eastern Sierra had long been used by the Pawaltis, or valley-dwellers. Mormon colonists established a western supply post at Genoa in 1851 that became known as Mormon Station. By the time of Rupert's birth in 1885, outsiders had appropriated nearly all Washoe lands, including the Genoa region. The men of Rupert's community worked as ranch hands, and the women, like his mother, were servants for white families.

During his childhood Rupert often met a bear in his dreams. When he gazed directly at the bear, it disappeared and young Rupert's body shot toward the moon. Bears, which held an especially powerful place in Washoe tradition, possessed supernatural powers. Rupert's older brother-in-law, Charlie Rube, explained: "If you talk about bear to anyone, the ground communicates your intentions to bear or the bear reads your mind. He concentrates on what you're thinking and knows. People among the Washoe can do the same thing, mostly doctors."

Rupert's dreams held a peculiar significance even in his early childhood. In 1892, for example, seven-year-old Rupert dreamed of his mother. At the time Susie John was mourning the death of a relative. In his dream Rupert saw his mother walk onto thin ice. Sometime after the dream, Susie John attempted suicide by walking onto an iced-over slough near the Carson River.[3]

Young Rupert spent most of his social time with his extended family. Charlie Rube and Rupert's uncle, Welewkushkush, played pivotal roles in his development. Although both men were referred to as doctors, Rube was actually an "antelope doctor" who engaged in hunting rather than healing. By the late nineteenth century very few animal doctors, also referred to as "charmers" or "bosses," remained. Some possessed the ability to attract deer and antelope. An early American observer, J. W. Hudson, encountered a charmer named "Old Tom" who in a trance "lay between two fires, into which he had caused certain herbs to charm the deer to him." Subsequent anthropologists portrayed a similar practice.

Stanley and Ruth Freed found individuals who used an herb called *mugálu* that could be used to put deer to sleep. James Downs also reported hearing about a sleeping medicine for deer.[4]

Antelope charmers such as Rube had a variety of responsibilities, including the maintenance of healthy herds. The charmer dreamed of a location where herds might be found and then visited the place when he awoke. If he saw signs of the animals, or the animals themselves, he instructed his kinsmen to build a corral with walls of sagebrush that would prevent the antelope from escaping. The charmer stood behind the corral and coaxed the antelope in. When the charm worked correctly, the antelope entered the corral "like sheep driven into a pen."[5]

Rupert's mentor Welewkushkush, the husband of Susie John's sister, was highly regarded for his shamanic powers. Young Rupert often watched his uncle work cures. He remembered one ceremony during which his uncle walked barefoot across fire without getting burned.[6] On another occasion Welewkushkush's young male apprentice fell severely ill on the shore of Lake Tahoe. Believing that a water being had taken the boy's soul, Welewkushkush began shaking his rattle and praying. He then walked into the lake until he was completely submerged. Witnesses claimed he remained underwater for ten minutes. When he returned, he circled the boy's body four times and told the apprentice's mother to shout the boy's name four times. As the boy regained consciousness his nose began to bleed, a sign that supernatural power had touched him. Welewkushkush turned the boy toward the lake and instructed him to shake the rattle. The boy was cured and acted as if he were waking from a dream.[7]

When not in the company of his older relatives Rupert spent much of his childhood alone, exploring the foothills of the eastern Sierra. He often encountered supernatural phenomena during his wanderings. On one occasion a cloudlike object brushed by him. Another time a nondescript white entity shadowed his movements along a desolate trail: when Rupert moved, it moved; when he stopped, it stopped. With in-creasing fear he approached the object, which turned out to be a piece of white linen snagged on a tree branch. Nevertheless, there was something magical about the experience, for the garment fluttered only when he moved.[8]

Another incident during Rupert's childhood brought him a new name. One day while hunting he wandered into a dry wash and a sudden flash flood threatened to sweep him away. When the dangerous waters reached him, they parted and raced by on either side. Word of the incident spread, and people began referring to Rupert as "Moses." Moses Street in Carson City took its name from Rupert.[9]

For the first eight years of his life Rupert enjoyed an informal education, learning from relatives and personal experience. But the federal government caught up with him in 1894. Along with thousands of Indian children across the United States, Rupert was forced to attend a government-run boarding school. By the end of the nineteenth century the wars with Native Americans were mostly over, and the U.S. government was looking for a "solution" to the "Indian problem." A former Army captain named Richard Henry Pratt offered an idea: change the Indians into "Americans." The country, he said, should "kill the Indian and save the man."

Pratt set up the first boarding school for Indians in 1879 at Carlisle, Pennsylvania. The children's hair was shorn, their clothes burned, and their culture expunged. The "success" of Carlisle brought a wave of boarding schools, especially across the West. The Carson Indian School, also called the Stewart Indian School, south of Carson City, opened its doors to thirty-seven Indian students on December 17, 1890.[10]

Using Carlisle as its model, the Carson Indian School provided pupils with basic academic lessons while emphasizing vocational and industrial training. The school's teachers worked hard to impose Euro-American gender roles on their students. Boys studied to become carpenters, printers, plumbers, and blacksmiths; girls focused on domestic responsibilities such as laundry, baking, sewing, and hygiene. Commissioner of Indian Affairs John H. Oberly clearly articulated this federal agenda in 1891 when he noted that he wanted school buildings to be converted into "homes" for the pupils where girls could learn how to "cook, to wash, to make and mend clothes, to sweep, to make beds—in short, . . . [be] instructed in all things that are taught to white girls in the homes of civilized communities." Indian boys, he suggested, should be taught farming and practical trades.[11]

The strictly regimented boarding-school environment proved a stark contrast to the freedom Rupert had enjoyed in the Sierra foothills. His experience likely paralleled that of other Washoe students. At the end of the twentieth century Roberta Snyder recalled the pain and trauma her parents, aunts, and uncles had suffered in boarding school when administrators forbade them from "speaking their own language, [and] . . . praying in their own ways."[12]

On his second day at school Rupert ran away. His escape violated rule 10E of the "Rules and Regulations of the Court of Indian Offenses at the Nevada Agency," which were enforceable by a specially empanelled Indian court. The rule stipulated: "Any parent or relative of a runaway pupil, or any other Indian, who shall harbor or protect said pupil knowing him to be a runaway, or who shall refuse to assist the police to secure the return of said pupil, is guilty of a misdemeanor, and upon conviction thereof, shall be punished by imprisonment in the Agency jail for a period not exceeding ten days or until such time as the pupil shall be returned to school."[13]

Rupert was returned to the school and wasted no time in making a second attempt. This time his escape earned him a violent whipping. That did not deter him, and a third unsuccessful attempt followed. Rupert finally accepted the inevitability of having to remain at school, but he did not allow it to extinguish his Washoe nature or quell his dreams.

In his fourth year at school Rupert experienced a power dream—his call to doctoring. He described the event in an interview in the 1960s: "I was sleeping in the school dormitory. I had a dream. I saw a buck in the west. It was a horned buck. It looked east. A voice said to me: 'Don't kill my babies anymore.' I woke up, and it was raining outside, and I had a nosebleed in bed." Rupert believed that the presence of a buck in the dream and the occurrence of rain revealed his ability to influence the weather, because the buck represented a "rain boss." The dream indicated that Rupert's primary power source, or wegeléyu, would be water. The buck's looking east served as a warning. The souls of bad people ended up in the east, and the buck was reminding Rupert that he could choose to do good or bad.[14]

Had officials at the Carson Indian School known of Rupert's growing power they would have monitored him closely. Traditional doctors were a prominent threat to the federal assimilation agenda. Rule 9C of the Nevada Indian Agency regulations stated: "The practice of the so called 'Medicine Man' or Indian doctor shall not be permitted on the reservation. Any Indian or Indians guilty of this offense shall be punished, upon conviction thereof, by imprisonment in the Agency jail for a period not less than 10 days, or until such time as the guilty person or persons shall give satisfactory evidence of intent to forever abandon the unlawful practice."[15]

Rupert remained at the Carson Indian School for nine years learning printing skills. At eighteen years old he began using his education to earn money as a typesetter for the *Reno Evening Gazette.* In his free time he studied "the science of suggestion"—hypnotism. After two years spent mastering this technique, Rupert became known for monthly sessions at which he would hypnotize people before members of the Reno Press Club. His skill was more than a parlor trick. Anthropologist and Rupert biographer Don Handelman noted that suggestions made by an Indian doctor during a healing ceremony were a critical component of the curing rites. Rupert, he wrote, was "an adept hypnotist" who used "such instruments as a rattle and eagle feather" to catch and hold his patient's attention. Rupert's hypnosis augmented the incantations, legerdemain, and other seemingly magical exhibitions that traditional doctors used to instill confidence in their curative skills.[16]

In 1907 Rupert's uncle, Welewkushkush, encouraged him to seek the guidance of another well-respected Washoe doctor, Beleliwe, known also as "Monkey Peter." A federal census taken in 1917 found sixty-year-old Beleliwe living a few miles from Genoa on the Springmeyer Ranch, near Minden, Nevada. Notes in the census margin refer to Beleliwe as "Doctor" and cite his year of birth as 1857. Beleliwe grew up among elders who knew a Washoe world undisturbed by American colonization. It is therefore likely that his teachers knew, and taught him, traditional methods of Washoe healing.[17]

Two Rupert contemporaries—prospective Washoe doctors John Frank and Sam Dick—also sought out Beleliwe for training and advice. John Frank referred to Beleliwe as "an honest Indian doctor" who "had the most power." He told an interviewer that Beleliwe worked with him long enough to determine that Frank should not become a doctor. Frank later described doctoring as too dangerous. "Old Indian doctors never lasted too long," he said.[18]

Sam Dick, who became Beleliwe's protégé, recalled a dangerous encounter with power. He had just bathed in a river. While lying in the sand to dry off he entered the dream state. A water being approached him and gave him a song. Dick recalled, "It showed me the way [to Cave Rock], like imagination." Next, the being departed for Cave Rock "in the water like ice all the way up the rock." In the days after that encounter the power began making him sick.

Beleliwe told Dick he would continue to be sick unless he "kept up" with his doctoring. "You can't get out of it unless you die," said Beleliwe.

Dick overcame his illness by following Beleliwe's directions. Six years later Dick experienced another traumatic incident involving a water being. Near Glenbrook, Nevada, some three miles north of Cave Rock, he walked out onto rocks near the water's edge. Hail began to fall, and Dick ran to an old cabin for cover. He rubbed his eyes to clear his vision and realized that he could not see. Dick believed the water being "didn't want me to see where he lived [and] . . . put me out of the way." Dick's blindness lasted three days. Following this incident Beleliwe told Dick what he had done wrong. Dick "should have gone down to the flat rocks, dived off into the water, and come up to the cave."[19]

Beleliwe recognized Rupert's potential and encouraged him to become a doctor. He began training his pupil on the use of his power, telling Rupert about incredible abilities of former Washoe doctors, such as an old woman who walked up the perpendicular side of a cliff. He described the feats of Welewkushkush walking under the water in Lake Tahoe. He told Rupert that "all kinds of sickness will look pretty tough, but it will melt; it seems like you can't do anything with it, but it will melt." By the end of his apprenticeship Rupert believed that Beleliwe was the most skilled doctor of his generation—"a great man" who "knew more than the rest put together." When anthropologist Robert Lowie spent time among Washoes in 1926, Rupert described Beleliwe to him as a "philosopher." Lowie described Rupert himself as "sophisticated" and a "mystic."[20]

Rupert was twenty-two when he healed his first patient. The mother of Rupert's good friend Frank Rivers had been in a deep depression following the death of her son, Rivers' brother. The family hired a non-Washoe doctor, who was unable to effect a cure. A few days after the attempted cure, Rupert wandered by her home and heard her crying. He went in and soothed the woman by cleaning her face and praying. She recovered within days, and word of the episode spread. In the months following his first cure Rupert acquired another power source to supplement water.

This second wegeléyu had nothing to do with Washoe tradition and raised concerns among older healers such as Welewkushkush. At the Carson City high school Rupert saw the skeleton of an East Indian Hindu man on display. He believed that at some point the spirit of the East Indian man entered him. In a dream the Hindu man asked to become Rupert's primary source of power. Two other dream figures—Indian women—protested. Rupert mediated by telling the opposing forces: "We all do the same work; let's help each other and be partners."[21]

In resolving the conflict Rupert had added to his healing power, but the resolution was a significant departure from methods used by traditional Washoe doctors. Rupert was the first to embrace a power source outside Washoe tradition, an example of his desire to expand his healing capabilities. He came to believe that power for all beings derived from a common "pool of energy." Those who were honest, faithful, and pure could tap into that pool regardless of their race, culture, or ethnicity.[22]

Two years passed before Rupert's next recorded cure, in 1909: a Washoe man suffering from typhoid fever who had been unsuccessfully treated by white doctors and other shamans. Rupert, sought out as a last resort because he was still a novice, cured the man, and word of Rupert's ability spread further among the Washoe. He continued to reside in Reno making a living in whatever ways he could.

In 1910, while working as a gardener for a banker, he began to suffer from pain in his muscles and joints. Rupert went to Welewkushkush, who ruled out physical ailments as the source of Rupert's pain. Instead he focused on his nephew's mind and behavior, and determined that Rupert's rheumatism resulted from his involvement in the "white world." Specifically, Welewkushkush claimed that Rupert had been studying from white books too much and drawing on the power of the non-Washoe Hindu spirit. He warned his nephew that if he continued to draw on non-Washoe sources for his healing, he would become sick and lose his power to heal. Although respectful of the renowned healer, Rupert continued breaking away from strict adherence to Washoe traditions.[23]

In a significant display of independence, Rupert married a Northern Paiute woman, Lizzie Smith, in the fall of 1910. The couple had met while attending school. Rupert's marriage to a non-Washoe demonstrated his recognition and acceptance of the changing world. Historically it was not unheard of for Washoes to marry Paiutes, but the practice was not encouraged during the early twentieth century. Lizzie's father, a skilled and well-known ranch hand, did not immediately approve of her choice. He had been a follower of Wovoka, "the Cutter"—the prophet and founder of the Ghost Dance that swept the West and the Great Plains during the late 1800s.

Rupert and Lizzie eventually had four children, and Rupert returned to work as a typesetter in Reno to support his family. By 1916 the family was living in Genoa. In December of that year John Pohland, a clerk for the U.S. Indian Service, sent Rupert a letter that reveals both a difficult marriage and the deep federal involvement in Washoe affairs during the early twentieth century. The clerk tersely informed Rupert about a complaint lodged against him which attested that Rupert had kicked his wife out of their home and that she was "having quite a hard time of it." Pohland ended the letter with a threat that "things could be made pretty hot for you" and encouraged Rupert to "make things right with her again."[24]

In his response to Pohland, dated February 8, 1917, Rupert did not address the complaint. Apparently Rupert and Lizzie had reconciled. Instead he asked whether or not Washoes were going to receive land around the Carson Valley. Although Indians were not "altogether helpless," he wrote, without land they had to rely on rations from the federal government. "I got a family of my own to look after, and I am always behind, going on credit." He closed by stating that although his sick mother occasionally received rations, she needed more help, too.[25]

The Washoe census conducted by the government in March 1917 recorded the Rupert family living at Wally's Hot Springs, close to Genoa. Included in the tally were Rupert's wife and three of their children: Harold, age six; Viola, age four; and Lily, ten months. His mother, Susanna, listed as seventy years old, was also living with Rupert.[26]

Rupert worked as a ranch hand to support his family while he continued to develop his healing practices. During this period state legislators and federal officials had begun to recognize the difficult conditions faced by Washoes, and in the previous year, 1916, secured small parcels for them in the Carson Valley, Carson City, and Reno. In 1924 Rupert left Genoa and took up land in the Carson colony, perhaps to be closer to his children who were at the Carson Indian School. He soon made his land profitable, maintaining an acre of strawberries and a flock of turkeys.

In 1933 Rupert's wife passed away and he entered a period characterized by deep meditations on metaphysics and healing. During this time Rupert began to develop a new cosmology that was based on "ethereal waves." Handelman likened these waves to "electric waves or pulses of energy." Rupert continued to believe that individuals could visit the spiritual dimension through dreams. He described three layers to the spirit world: a coarse layer, a refined layer, and a pure layer where the creator or omnipotent being exists.

Rupert followed the traditional Washoe cosmology in believing that all beings contain energy, but he suggested that this energy came from the third layer. He described an essence of power in the spiritual world that facilitates all healing—the same power Jesus Christ used to perform the miracles described in the New Testament. Christ, Old Testament prophets, and shamans employed the same source of power, Rupert explained. "The power is ever present; it never wears out."[27]

With his new cosmology and system of healing, Rupert attracted patients from various ethnic groups. While working with Rupert in the summer of 1964, Handelman learned about forty-one healing sessions stretching back to 1907. The cases did not represent an inclusive list, but Handelman's description illustrates their diversity. Rupert healed a young Washoe who, believing he had polio was unable to walk; a Shoshone boy with auditory hallucinations that caused him to think three men were trying to kill him; a Protestant minister suffering from migraine headaches; a Mexican woman in Sacramento who was diagnosed by doctors as having a malignant tumor of the abdomen; and a World War II veteran whose hallucinations that German soldiers were trying to strangle him with barbed wire caused him to lacerate his own neck. He also restored the health of a white storekeeper with heart problems. The storekeeper, who lived seventy-five miles away in Fallon, Nevada, claimed he would never again see a doctor other than Rupert.[28]

Handelman noted that Rupert believed that reality in healing is situational; that is, it involves individual perception and "psychological set." Rupert knew that his meditations and dialogues with spirits appeared strange to those uninitiated in the ways of shamanic power. "You don't know what I am talking about," he commented to Handelman, "and the same is true for anybody who reads this thing you write. What is real for me is not real for you."[29]

Late in his life, after four days and nights of vision seeking and dreaming, Rupert healed a seriously ill Hawaiian who was also a curer. For his effort Rupert received another source of power: a Hawaiian spirit helper. One of the things Rupert learned from this new source was that "everything comes quick and goes away quick." He took this to mean that instead of taking several days, he could utilize techniques selected for a particular case and effect the cure in a matter of hours or even a few minutes. He continued to adapt throughout his life, relinquishing ceremonial rites he had used for nearly fifty years when a new method promised better results.[30] At the end of his life, true to his philosophy regarding exposing his healing practices, Rupert said, "I don't really do nothing but help nature."[31]

Despite his reluctance to discuss it, Rupert's power continues to resonate in the eastern Sierra. The Forest Service's final decision about Cave Rock directly acknowledged Rupert's legacy and his influence as a consultant in the field of anthropology. The agency also noted his importance as an innovator who maintained a balance between tradition and experimentation. Indeed, the Forest Service decided to manage the site to reflect "prehistory through the year of Henry Rupert's death."[32]

FIVE

Slayer

The brief history of rock climbing at Cave Rock is replete with accomplishments featuring the development of challenging and spectacular routes. Even before the Washoe sacred site issue came to the fore, the site's enthusiasts faced a problem that confronts all modern climbers: they value new climbs and first ascents, but each achievement reduces this finite resource. The supply of high-quality, accessible rock for climbing is exhaustible, and demand for it has grown immeasurably.[1]

A Forest Service survey conducted in 1995 revealed that 7 million U.S. citizens participated in rock climbing in 1994–95 (with an additional 9.5 million participating in mountain climbing), and estimated that 100,000 people try rock climbing for the first time every year. The rock-climbing community, formerly small and independent, has evolved into something resembling "a national subculture" with a common language and values. Although the group is spread across the country, its members share a lifestyle and are surprisingly homogeneous: they read the same three or four journals and visit the same major climbing areas.[2]

In the 1950s the climbing community viewed both free climbing, in which ropes are used for safety only, and aided climbs as acceptable. By the early 1970s free climbing had become the only acceptable method of ascent. Reacting to thirty years' worth of piton scars left in Yosemite and other once pristine sites, free climbers insisted on minimizing the number of bolts placed in the rock. A widely disseminated magazine article published in 1973 summarized free climbers' complaint about sport climbing: "The mere act of achieving a route has become secondary, while the style in which a route is achieved has become of primary importance."[3] The community extolled the personal rewards of overcoming hardships, challenge, and exertion as opposed to competition, which was seen as egotistical.

In the early 1980s the biggest ethical issue for rock climbers was whether or not they should use gymnasts' chalk on their hands. The question of environmental and aesthetic damage caused by climbers had yet to arise. By 1985 French climbers had rap-bolted the Verdon Gorge, igniting the idea of accessing all parts of rock faces rather than only their crack systems.[4] Traditionalists viewed the new sport climbing as overly competitive and environmentally destructive. They continued to advocate "clean" climbing using removable pieces of protection, and argued vehemently against overconsumption of the resource. As the anchors and slings of sport climbers began to cover rock faces, complaints—some by traditionalists, others by wilderness devotees—were taken to public land regulatory agencies. Land managers began to count bolts.

An October 1993 *Los Angeles Times* article reported that the U.S. Park Service, fearing irreversible environmental damage, was seeking regulations to limit what climbers could do. Climbers argued that prohibiting the placement of new bolts and the replacement of old, weakened ones—fundamental to climber safety—would put them in jeopardy. They did not want to use top ropes because that would remove the sport's key appeal: climbing with as little assistance as possible. Climbing guidebooks promoted environmental ethics and restraint as well as skill and integrity in putting up routes—creating lines only if they differed significantly in character from those nearby. Route builders were asked to limit their bolts and to use rock-matching colors for bolt hangers, webbing, and chalk.

In 1997 the Leave No Trace organization produced a document that went much further and urged rock climbers to leave sacred sites alone: "Disturbing cultural sites may render them useless for study and observation in the future, and shows disregard for early American cultures."[5] By that time, however, a great deal of damage had already been done. The rock climbers who created the original routes at Cave Rock had no qualms in this regard because the site had not been publicly identified as a cultural site.

Climbers began securing bolts for sport climbing in the crags around Lake Tahoe in the mid-1980s. Boldness, difficulty, and danger have always been key components of a climb; if the route has the additional quality of being aesthetically pleasing, it becomes particularly valued. Few places could match the steep walls of Cave Rock towering above Lake Tahoe in all of those factors.[6]

Route builders, who determine the difficulty factor of a particular climbing route, rate it by the most difficult technical move in the climb, although the rating may go up if the climb calls for exceptional endurance. On the Yosemite Scale used throughout the western United States, routes that require securing ropes and utilizing a belayer (who stands below and assists the climber by maintaining the correct tension on the rope) range in difficulty from 5.0 to 5.15. Routes rated above 5.1 are accompanied by letters (a–d) that further quantify difficulty. As of 2005 the most difficult climbs gaining worldwide consensus were rated at 5.15a. Controversy surrounds the ratings of the two highest-ranked routes in the world. One in France converted to the Yosemite Scale as 5.15b, and another in Spain as 5.15c. By summer 1992, Cave Rock, with its extreme overhang, had seven routes rated at least 5.13.[7]

Rebecca Noyes, a skilled climber from Reno, described the appeal of climbing in an interview: "In terms of going up there for the thrill or terror, or being terribly endangered, that's not what we do. In terms of jumping off the top just for the sheer fun of it, that's not really what we do. The thing about climbing is not that it's just a physical challenge but that it's a mental challenge. It's facing your own capabilities and trying to figure out how you, as different from any other climber, are going to make it from the bottom to the top of the route." She described climbing at Cave Rock as a quiet, introspective, respectful activity that may not be quite as exciting as the public perceives it, but is instead more important to the individual.[8] Noyes clearly was not talking about the climber most often identified with Cave Rock.

By 1992 Dan Osman had created four of the seven highest-rated routes at Cave Rock, and it was he who paved the cave floor. His mother, a horse trainer and two-time world champion rodeo barrel rider, had encouraged him to begin rock climbing at the age of twelve. His Japanese-American father had been a police officer for more than twenty years and worked as part of a SWAT team. As a boy Dan studied aikido and kung fu, and his father trained him in the bushido ethic of his samurai ancestors: the way of the warrior that reveres loyalty, self-discipline, and respectful and ethical behavior. The younger Osman was built like a gymnast. With his long hair and rugged good looks he was frequently mistaken for a Native American.

Osman paid the rent for whatever room or studio he occupied with the small amounts he earned from climbing sponsors, teaching or guiding climbing, and periodic work as a carpenter. He wanted to sustain himself entirely through climbing endeavors, and for a long time he made only enough to support his climbing and contribute to the upkeep of his daughter, Emma, who lived with her mother in Gardnerville, Nevada. Osman's doctor, an orthopedic surgeon and fellow climber, sometimes accepted sponsors' gear in lieu of payment for treating Osman's broken bones.

Osman's meager budget did not allow for speeding tickets and unregistered vehicle and illegal parking fines. Even as his earnings rose—when photographs and movies of his exploits gained him fame, and sponsors and advertisers sought him out—his vehicle violation fees went unpaid. Now in his thirties, he still liked street racing and received three speeding tickets in a single weekend after buying a new truck.[9]

His friends, many of them rock climbers, joked about "Dano-time," as they referred to his chronic lateness to appointments. Part of the difficulty was caused by his personable nature. He would stop and talk with anyone. His friend Andrew Todhunter, a fellow climber who wrote a book about Osman, described a typical exchange that took place when a woman who had seen a television program about Dan came to his table in a restaurant.

"Yeah, it's definitely you. . . . I told my husband it was you," she said. "We were so impressed. . . . I could never imagine doing that."

"It's just what I do," [said] Osman. "If you put me in your job, I'm sure I'd feel exactly the same way."

"Do you get scared, doing those things?"

"Yeah. All the time."[10]

Osman would take as much time discussing climbing with a novice as he would with expert friends. "His regret is so apparently sincere," Todhunter commented after waiting for Osman for an entire day, "that I find myself feeling more sympathy for Osman's forgetfulness than personal offense at its effects." His mother's nickname for him growing up, "Danny I forgot," described his adult life as well.[11]

Osman's climbing feats became legendary in the 1990s. Filmmakers captured him making numerous daredevil climbs: free-soloing (climbing without any safety apparatus) up a sheer rock face with a rating of 5.11 where a misstep would mean death; leaping to catch a crack at the top of a route; hurdling to a narrow crag across a deep abyss; scrambling, nearly running, up faces ranging in difficulty from 5.6 to 5.11c. During the same period he also became renowned for his route building.[12]

Because it might require months, and "a first ascent can never be repeated," Osman took particular care in placing a new route and saw its completion as a historic accomplishment. In 1990 Osman, along with Paul Crawford and Dimitri Barton, had completed a route at Cave Rock called "Port of Entry," rated at 5.12a. That same year Osman took nine months to complete a line called "Psycho Monkey," rated 5.13a. At the time he believed it was the hardest route possible at the cave.[13] He later described how he came to build other lines: "When I finished [Psycho Monkey], I looked to the right and saw the line of 'Phantom Lord,' which was harder [5.13b]. When I finished that, I looked to the right again and saw the 5.14 I'm working on now. One day, while I was working on that, I saw the line of 'Slayer.' At the time I thought it was going to be harder than all of them. I yelled to my belayer to lower me, and ran over to start working on it."[14]

Climbing magazine labeled "Slayer," which merited a 5.13d/5.14a rating, his "grand" project." It took thirteen months to complete and was originally rated 5.14a, but two expert climbers found easier sequences and downgraded it. Others since have concurred with the original rating. Building "Slayer" took so long because Osman built routes from the ground up as opposed to rap-bolting (rappeling down to set the bolts), an easier and faster technique. Climbing to establish a line is seen as valuing tradition, and Osman took extreme care to create spare, graceful lines. A serious injury incurred when Osman fell while working at the route's run-out also delayed the route's completion. When Osman's rope did not have the requisite slack, the belayer instinctively leaned back, propelling Osman at tremendous speed into the rock and breaking both his ankles.[15]

During his convalescence Osman spent three hundred hours paving the Cave Rock floor. He moved boulders with a come-along winch hooked to bolts in the cave walls. Hundreds of bags of cement and countless buckets of water were hauled along the narrow pathway up to the cave. He rearranged the gravel and rockfall and set flat stones, seamed with mortar, as flooring. After his efforts the cave had the look of an elegant lakefront terrace. It included a low rock wall on the outer edge, steps into the cave, and boulders propped up as freeform belay benches that could be used for changing shoes, eating, or relaxing in the sun. The floor was described as having a "sort of Zen garden effect." Some locals complained because Osman's improvements attracted more climbers. After that, Osman said, he often thought of tearing it all out again.[16]

Falling and being caught by the safety rope is an integral part of sport climbing, in particular when an expert route is being built. Two years earlier, when Osman established his line for "Phantom Lord," he fell time after time while searching for hand placements in the overhanging rock—as many as fifty falls attempting to set one bolt. Although he was secured by his rope, each fall caused a jolt of fear. Osman eventually concluded that falling, not climbing, was the ultimate thrill.

Osman had reached the pinnacle of the climbing culture at this point. He was a celebrity. The North Face climbing team recruited him to join "a collection of the world's foremost rock climbers and alpinists." But his goals were changing. At Cave Rock he began studying and practicing falling while tethered with the rope.[17] He made adventure videos and MTV commercials of his single-rope jumps from other rocks, bridges, and cliffs. Osman's plunges got progressively longer: 50 feet, 250 feet, and eventually 1,000 feet. While making the extreme sport videos he secured contracts to test ropes and rigging for companies that manufacture climbing gear. Seemingly more important, he was pushing the limits of his courage. Todhunter commented: "Osman does not turn his back to fear. He tracks it, baits it, and withstands its rush." Osman's father at first disapproved of his son's climbing career but came to admire his feats. "In climbing he found something where he could test himself against himself," his father said. "He met the tiger and he didn't run. He walked away."[18]

Osman's spectacular falls were edgier and less easily explained as sport. Hundreds of thousands of people have watched the falls on television, YouTube, and videos. He stands on the edge of a cliff, hundreds of feet above a canyon and, after a countdown, steps briskly off; or he back-flips, swan dives, rides a bicycle, or skateboards off. Turning, somersaulting, or twisting during shorter falls, he bounces and swings when the rope reaches its end.

"Yeahhh! Yoohoo! Holy sister! Oh man! Yeahhh! What a rush that is," Osman exclaimed after a record-setting thousand-foot fall. On that jump he had to adjust his body to steer away from the rock wall and end at an opening between tree tops. He was filmed cartwheeling off Cave Rock, the rope catching him just as he touched the rock-filled water of the lake.

In another setting he hung, batlike, from a bridge hundreds of feet in the air before dropping head first. He studied sky divers and acrobatic ski jumpers to learn how to position his body and spread the load of impact. Before jumps he stretched the rope and designed elaborate and intricate anchor, rope, and pulley systems to lessen the shock when the rope played out.[19]

Osman's climbs and falls at Cave Rock were interrupted when the Forest Service issued its temporary closure order in February 1997, three and a half years after the Washoe tribe had first asked the government to act. Ownership status questions had to be resolved between the Forest Service, the Nevada Department of Transportation, and the Nevada State Parks system, each of whom had certain jurisdictional responsibilities. In December 1994 the Forest Service determined that the portion of the area including Cave Rock came under its management.[20] Once that was decided, Forest Service personnel studied the site and found that it met requisites for nomination to the National Register of Historic Places.

In 1996 President Bill Clinton signed two executive orders that influenced the issue of Cave Rock. Executive Order 13006 reaffirmed the government's commitment to historic preservation leadership and called on federal agencies to partner with Indian tribes and others to enhance the preservation program. Executive Order 13007, often called the Indian Sacred Sites Executive Order, stipulated that federal land managers must accommodate access to and ceremonial use of Indian sacred sites by Indian religious practitioners; and must also avoid adversely affecting the physical integrity of such sites. The order directed that the head of each executive branch agency involved must report within a year on its implementation. Washoe Tribal Chair Brian Wallace wrote Robert Harris, the forest supervisor for Lake Tahoe, on August 13, 1996, reiterating the tribe's strong objection to the adverse effects of recreation activities on what they considered their sacred site.

Harris, whose retirement was imminent, had begun his Forest Service career as an engineer. He was well regarded in the agency, and other forest supervisors were always willing to listen to him. He took two actions. He sent a letter to the Nevada historic preservation officer requesting comment on the property's eligibility for the National Register of Historic Places, and he issued the closure order. The Nevada preservation officer wrote back two weeks later affirming the site's eligibility.

In accommodating Washoe concerns, Harris cited EO 13007 and two statutes: the 1966 National Historic Preservation Act, which directed federal agencies to act as stewards of the nation's historic properties; and the American Indian Religious Freedom Act, which set federal policy for protecting the rights of American Indians to exercise their traditional religions, including access to sacred sites. The temporary closure was to be in effect until the end of the year, "the minimum period required to complete a comprehensive management plan for the Cave Rock area."[21]

At the end of February 1997 Dan Osman joined eighteen other incensed climbers at a South Tahoe climbers' gym to discuss Harris' decision. The group's knowledge about the situation was a mixture of facts and misinformation. They had heard a baseless rumor that the Forest Service was receiving a valuable piece of land from the Washoes in exchange for Cave Rock. Some mistakenly believed that the Washoes originally sold their land at Lake Tahoe for a penny an acre and had no right to reclaim it. In the climbers' view, the tribe was belatedly attempting to reclaim the rock after having abandoned it for decades. Some questioned the Washoes' motives; others accused the Forest Service of corruption.

Osman calmly addressed the group. "The Washoe had their time in the cave," he said. "This is our time. When we started climbing there, the cave was a mess—full of beer bottles and diapers and garbage. Where were the Washoe then? We cleaned it up, and we treat it with respect. The Washoe say it is a spiritual place for them. But it's a spiritual place for us, too. Anyone who climbs can understand that." He told the others that he would meet with the Washoes, and that he had a good feeling about it. "Once they understand how we feel about the cave," he said, "I think we can work something out."[22]

The Forest Service lifted the closure order at Cave Rock three months after it went into effect. Supervisor Robert Harris had been replaced, and the new supervisor, under legal pressure from the Access Fund, had rescinded the order.[23]

A year and a half later, in October 1998, Dan Osman traveled to Yosemite Valley to attempt a record jump from the rock named Leaning Tower. He had been serious and introspective in an earlier interview. His nearly waist-length hair and striking, square features marked him as an extreme sport superstar. He spoke of taking some time off: "It's just a matter of time before things maybe start catching up with you," he said, "and I've got this really hardcore group of guardian angels that need a prepaid vacation." In Yosemite, after placing the anchors and setting the ropes, he got a call from his daughter, who was upset and wanted to see him. He left the setup and went to Gardnerville.

When Osman returned to Yosemite two days later, authorities arrested him for several vehicle violations, some of them federal because they occurred in a national park. When he was finally released on bond after fourteen days in jail, he returned to Nevada with his sister and brother-in-law. After getting word that park rangers were threatening to confiscate his gear, which was still on the rocks, he got a friend to drive him back. Once there, he refused to let the hard work and creativity of setting the rig go to waste. In the late afternoon of November 23 he made a jump of some 925 feet. Darkness was settling in as he added 75 feet so he could jump using more than 1,000 feet of line. The additional length changed the angle of the jump and placed undue pressure on one of the knots. He jumped, the line snapped, and Osman fell to his death.

More than two hundred friends gathered to watch five days later as his ashes were spread over Lake Tahoe at Cave Rock.[24]

Cave Rock, "De' ek wadapush" in Washoe, is the 360-foot core remnant of a volcano that erupted three million years ago. This view, from the west taken in the early 1900s, shows the main cave above and to the right of the trestle bridge, barely noticeable on the lower left of the rock. Courtesy Special Collections, University of Nevada, Reno, Library.

View from the north side of Cave Rock featuring its lower portion. Notice the silhouette of the Lady of the Lake in the formation and the one-way trestle bridge—the only thing that stood between "drivers and eternity." Photo taken in 1911 by Harold A. Parker. Courtesy Special Collections, University of Nevada, Reno, Library.

Freight wagons pause for a photo below the main cave after the precipitous trip around Cave Rock in the 1860s. Courtesy Special Collections, University of Nevada, Reno, Library.

View of Cave Rock from the south. Close scrutiny shows the first tunnel blasted through the rock in 1931. Courtesy Special Collections, University of Nevada, Reno, Library.

Postcard (detail) from 1910 featuring Cave Rock and the trestle bridge. Courtesy Special Collections, University of Nevada Reno, Library.

Close-up of the first tunnel from the north side, taken in the 1930s. Courtesy Special Collections, University of Nevada, Reno, Library.

Although Lake Tahoe had largely been privatized by the early twentieth century, Washoes continued to spend summer months there, often working for tourist resorts (note the Al Tahoe Inn sign in upper right). This photo from the early 1900s shows Captain Pete Mayo (*fourth from left*) and his wife, Sarah Mayo, with baskets. Captain Pete likely acted as a fishing guide for white tourists while his wife marketed her baskets. Courtesy Special Collections, University of Nevada, Reno, Library.

One of the only public photos of Henry "Moses" Rupert. Rupert is the young man in the back to the right. Pete and Sarah May, the governor of Nevada, Emmet D. Boyle, and Washoe leader Hank Pete stand in front. Washoe leader Ben James appears next to Rupert. Courtesy Special Collections, University of Nevada, Reno, Library.

Jason Campbell, pictured here, built one of two routes with the extreme difficulty rating of 14A at Cave Rock. Campbell is high above the lake on a route called "Bone Crusher." Courtesy Jim Thornburg.

Dan Osman making one of his jumps at Yosemite, where he ultimately lost his life in November 1998. Courtesy Jim Thornburg.

John Dayberry below the highway at Cave Rock, summer 2009. He is using an extension, or "cheat stick," to pull himself to the rock to remove anchors. Note the safety lines and the five-gallon bucket holding his tools. Courtesy John Dayberry.

SIX

Hunter-Gatherers and Courts

The Washoes had very little reason to hope for a favorable outcome if their attempt to halt climbing at Cave Rock was taken into the court system. Prior to the last decade of the twentieth century, no Native American sacred site claim had ever been upheld in a federal court. While Christian sites such as Catholic missions and the National Cathedral in Washington, D.C., gained protection as national monuments, Native sites continued to be exploited, developed, and destroyed.

Euro-Americans have ignored Native property rights from the time of earliest contact. Because at first the Natives themselves had no understanding of the American concept of landownership, the newcomers identified them as "hunter-gatherers" who had a transitory and impermanent relationship with specific sites. European immigrants simply appropriated the lands they coveted, either failing to recognize the sort of communal ownership the Indians practiced or placing no value on it.[1]

In 1823 Chief Justice John Marshall issued what would become a landmark ruling on the subject. In the case of *Johnson v. M'Intosh,* the Court had to decide on the legal ownership of a piece of land. One of the parties to the suit had purchased the land from Indians; the other had been given a patent of ownership for the land by the federal government. The Court ruled in favor of the latter, writing that the Indians had never owned the land, and thus had no right to sell it. Marshall ruled that the United States, as a Christian nation, had inherited from England title to all property in North America previously unclaimed by a Western nation. Indians had the right to occupy land but could not own it. Since *M'Intosh* the courts have consistently found for state interests, which have often involved financial promotion, over Native American religious values.[2]

Courts base their findings on precedent, and tens of thousands of property cases define recognized property rights. G. Jon Roush, president of the Wilderness Society, termed such rulings "the cover of law" when he urged Congress in 1994 to protect sacred Indian sites. In his dissent against the majority ruling in *Lyng v. Northwest Indian Cemetery Protective Association* in 1988, Supreme Court Justice William J. Brennan Jr. pointed out that rather than balancing the competing viewpoints of Western culture and Native Americans, the court was both finding against the Native peoples and establishing unassailable precedent for the future. "The Court," he wrote, "has effectively bestowed on one party to this conflict the unilateral authority to resolve all future disputes in its favor, subject only to the Court's toothless exhortation to be 'sensitive' to affected religions. In my view, however, Native Americans deserve—and the Constitution demands—more than this." Only two justices joined in Brennan's dissent.[3]

The courts' reasoning has always centered on economic concerns and the issue of the government's control of federal lands. Glen Canyon Dam, built in 1963 to create Lake Powell, flooded a Navajo prayer site. After the dam was finished, the Bureau of Reclamation raised the water level behind it until the water entered Bridge Canyon, another important religious and cultural feature. The higher water level gave tourists easier access to the tribe's sacred Rainbow Bridge. Earlier the Park Service had licensed boat tours; now it promoted other activities around the bridge. When the Court finally heard the tribe's appeal in 1977, it found for the federal land managers despite its favorable view of the Navajos' religious arguments. The interests of the tribe simply did not measure up when weighed against the economic prosperity produced by Glen Canyon Dam.[4]

Native American religious sites encompass lands used for ceremonies, prayer, vision quests, gravesites, and places such as Cave Rock where shamans work with power.[5] The fact that there are tens of thousands of these sites and that they include vast expanses continues to cause problems in acknowledging and preserving them. But even when only a small property is at stake, the federal government tends not to give up control. The government determines whether an area should be open to the public, open to development, or protected as a historic site.

Government interests that have been awarded precedence over Native American religious concerns include logging, road building, flood control, navigation, electric power generation, the construction of an observatory, and recreational uses including skiing. In the case of the observatory, Mount Graham in Arizona, the San Carlos Apaches objected because the mountaintop is the site where deities gave the people their original medicine. The court found that the argument had merit but was filed too late. The delay was the result of the failure of the several tribes concerned to agree who would speak for them. By the time the San Carlos Apaches presented their case, the decision-making process had advanced too far to be reversed.

The skiing lawsuit involved a government-owned resort on land in the San Francisco Peaks in Arizona that is sacred to both the Hopi and Navajo tribes. The ski resort wanted to expand; the Hopis and Navajos were opposed. The Hopis' chairman testified that activity at that site undermined the tribe's cultural foundation. "If the ski resort remains or is expanded," he said, "our people will not accept the view that this is the sacred Home of the Kachinas. The basis of our existence as a society will become a mere fairy tale to our people." The court ruled against the Hopis and upheld the resort's right to pursue recreational improvements. The reasoning, which would be mirrored in an early Forest Service decision at Cave Rock, concluded that developing and expanding the ski area did not deny tribal access to the mountain peaks and was thus acceptable.[6]

Native Americans' petitions to the court have been dismissed on one of two grounds: either the state's interests superseded the tribe's, as in the cases of Rainbow Bridge, San Francisco Peaks, and—as the Access Fund would propose—Cave Rock; or the tribe could not demonstrate that the site was central to its religious practice. Proving the latter can be especially onerous—or impossible—because nearly all Native American cultures are based on oral tradition, which is often considered hearsay in a court of law. Further, Native religions generally have no rigid hierarchy of importance, and their "central" beliefs are not as easy to evaluate as those of Western religions. Thus in the case of *Sequoyah v. Tennessee Valley Authority* the Sixth Circuit Court held that flooding a valley containing numerous sacred sites was constitutional because the tribe lacked evidence of the sites' centrality to religious observance.[7]

Court cases brought by Native communities in the second half of the twentieth century were based on the First Amendment, which states that "Congress shall make no law respecting an establishment of religion, or prohibiting the free exercise thereof." The first part of the amendment, commonly referred to as the Establishment Clause, prohibits the government from passing legislation to establish an official religion or from promoting one religion over another. The second part, known as the Free Exercise Clause, stipulates that the government must accommodate religious practices.

Native peoples contended that the desecration or destruction of their sacred sites abrogated the free exercise of their religion. In 1978, seeking to strengthen Native claims, Congress passed the American Indian Religious Freedom Act, which acknowledged prior infringements and declared: "Henceforth it shall be the policy of the United States to protect and preserve for American Indians their inherent right to freedom to believe, express, and exercise the traditional religions of the American Indian, Eskimo, Aleut, and Native Hawaiians, including but not limited to access to sites, use and possession of sacred objects, and the freedom to worship through ceremonial and traditional rites." But in 1981 a district court judge ruled that the act "was meant to insure that the American Indians were given the protection that they are guaranteed under the First Amendment; it was not meant to in any way grant them rights in excess of those guarantees." No court has since granted the act weight beyond that ruling, and judgments have continued to favor nontribal interests.[8]

In a 1988 case that effectively ended the First Amendment venue as a possible safeguard, the Supreme Court indicated another path that might be used to protect sacred sites, one that would be critical in the Cave Rock case: government agency policy. *Lyng v. Northwest Indian Cemetery Protective Association* concerned a traditional Native cemetery and a site for religious rituals, both in the Six Rivers National Forest in northern California. The Rehnquist Court heard the case after the Forest Service approved a paved road through the cemetery and timber harvesting in an area near the religious site. The lower courts had found for the Indians, saying the site was both central and indispensable to their religious practice. The Rehnquist Court overturned the finding, ruling that the only limitations on the government were that it not coerce any group into violating its religious beliefs or penalize it for practicing them.

Sandra Day O'Conner wrote the majority decision, noting that lawful government actions do not require compelling justification when they do not pressure individuals to act contrary to their beliefs. She concluded that the Free Exercise Clause delineates what the government cannot do, not what individuals might exact from the government. "Even assuming that the Government's actions here will virtually destroy the Indians' ability to practice their religion," she wrote, "the Constitution simply does not provide a principle that could justify upholding respondents' legal claims." Although the ruling was an otherwise devastating finding for Native Americans, O'Conner did concede that the government's right to use its own land "should not discourage it from accommodating religious practices like those engaged in by the Indian respondents."[9]

Although the *Lyng* decision was further evidence that the courts would not protect sacred Indian interests, other forces set in motion in the tumultuous 1960s and 1970s were at work. Indian communities throughout North America publicized injustices through fish-ins, protests, and powwows. The seizure of Alcatraz Island in 1969 by a group calling itself Indians of All Tribes symbolized the emergence of Indian networks poised to challenge stereotypes and promote the redress of injustices. The movement included tribal lobbying of Congress and an academic shift that initiated Indian-run community colleges and American Indian studies programs at state colleges and universities.[10]

These activities accentuated the courts' failure to protect Indian rights and convinced Congress that other legislative measures were needed. In 1992 Congress amended the National Historic Preservation Act and charged federal agencies to ensure better representation of Native peoples' interests. The Religious Freedom Restoration Act, passed in 1993, included as one of its statements of purpose: "Governments should not substantially burden religious exercise without compelling justification."

In 1994 President Bill Clinton weighed in. At a historic White House meeting with Native Americans he presented an executive memorandum that established an interagency working group to share information and provide a forum for resolution of issues regarding Indian policy. In 1996 Clinton issued the executive order directing federal agencies to accommodate practitioners' access to sacred sites and protect the sites' physical integrity. Neither the legislative acts nor the executive actions called for vigorous enforcement (Clinton's order was to be implemented only "to the extent practicable"). Although they lacked teeth, the actions played an essential role in establishing federal agencies' responsibilities regarding Native sites, customs, and religious practices.[11]

Agencies that manage lands, in particular the Park Service and Bureau of Land Management of the Department of the Interior, and the U.S. Department of Agriculture's Forest Service, are charged with balancing public uses within their jurisdictions. The Park Service has to weigh decisions for providing public access against its mandate to conserve and preserve the resources under its jurisdiction. The other two agencies are multiple-use entities charged with the responsibility for allowing logging, mining, grazing, and oil and gas drilling as well as public use and preservation. This need to consider competing activities makes the process for determining usage extremely complicated.

At the same time these agencies have greater freedom than the courts because they are not constrained by the precedents that limit judicial decision making. The legislation mentioned above and President Clinton's executive orders led to large-scale policies that allowed fairer consideration of Indian claims. Because the federal agencies handle only site-specific cases, their decisions are limited in scope and consequences with regard to national policy—and are more likely to be upheld by the courts.[12] Once upheld, a decision sets precedence. This fact affected the Cave Rock case because the Access Fund and other advocacy groups had to decide how far in the court system they would appeal, fearing the legal consequences of a circuit court or Supreme Court ruling against them.

The most publicized dispute in agency decision making in the 1990s also dealt with climbing at a sacred site and had an enormous influence on the Cave Rock fight. The disagreement was over use at the nation's first national monument, Devil's Tower/Bear Lodge, which was dedicated by President Theodore Roosevelt in 1906. Devil's Tower is a unique column of rock that was formed by lava boiling out of the earth's molten core. The Lakotas, Cheyennes, and Kiowas call the tower "Bear Lodge" and consider it a religious place of refuge. An important story in Kiowa mythology tells that the tower was formed when a giant bear chased seven young girls onto the rock. The girls prayed for help, and the rock was lifted heavenward, out of the bear's reach. When it reached the sky the girls became the stars of the Big Dipper. The great striations on the rock today show where the bear's claws scarred the rising rock.

The first recorded climb of Devil's Tower/Bear Lodge by Euro-Americans took place in 1893. Routes were established in the 1930s. In the 1980s sport climbers began inserting bolts in the rock, and by the last part of the twentieth century the column had become one of the best rock-climbing sites in the world.

The site's Native users complained that the climbers were interfering with their rites, most especially during the summer solstice in the month of June. In the late 1990s the Park Service, in a process later used by the Forest Service in its attempt to resolve the Cave Rock issue, held meetings between tribal representatives and climbers' groups. The Park Service meetings, which included county commissioners and environmentalists, led to a consensus determining that climbing would be allowed with three stipulations: no new routes would be established, equipment had to be camouflaged, and a voluntary ban—for those who wished to adhere to the tribes' request—was to be instituted during the month of June. The Park Service reserved the right to revisit the issue if the voluntary closure proved ineffective in limiting climbing.[13]

The original Park Service order suspended the issuance of commercial climbing licenses in June. When a Wyoming district court judge blocked the plan, deeming the June suspension order to be a violation of the Establishment Clause, the Park Service superintendent issued a new order removing the June license restriction. In June 1998, when 85 percent of the climbers who ordinarily used the rock stayed away, a defiant minority climbed in full view of Lakota sun dancers during their solstice ceremony.[14]

Those who climbed that day wanted the courts to reverse even the voluntary June moratorium. They were supported in their efforts by the ultra-conservative Mountain States Legal Foundation, a litigation and advocacy group known for its attacks on environmental protection policies. Much of the foundation's litigation has been on behalf of oil, mineral, development, and timber interests. The plaintiffs in the Devil's Tower/Bear Lodge complaint demanded the removal of any mention of tribal religion in publications and interpretive signage at the site as well as a permanent injunction against the voluntary June restriction. The foundation's lawyers argued that because the Park Service might take further action against climbing if the voluntary closure proved ineffective, the moratorium was in fact involuntary. The trial court and the Tenth Circuit Court of Appeals did not find that the interpretive information was indoctrinating or coercing visitors toward Native religions. They ruled that the religious accommodation complied with the Free Exercise Clause of the First Amendment, removing obstacles to religious observance, rather than violating the Establishment Clause by encouraging such observance. Further, the courts found the moratorium argument speculative, although their decisions noted that an involuntary ban would likely be unconstitutional.[15]

The Devil's Tower/Bear Lodge settlement, however burdensome for the tribes and imperfect for climbers, showed a federal agency's willingness to develop a compromise in a land dispute. It also ignited reactions from groups such as the Jefferson 21st Century Institute. That organization, which is "dedicated to the separation of religion and government," issued a statement portraying Park Service employees as a quasi militia: "Americans desiring to enter upon otherwise unrestricted public lands should not have to face uniformed gun-packing government employees asking them to 'voluntarily' stay away in respect of other's religious beliefs." William Perry Pendley, the president of the Mountain States Legal Foundation, argued that the Park Service was enforcing "a religious orthodoxy" because it was trying to make all visitors "show respect" for Native religion.[16] The settlement remained despite these groups' protests.

In 2001 the Mountain States Legal Foundation joined another case against an Indian sacred site. A timber company, Wyoming Sawmills, had filed suit against the Forest Service to challenge the agency's decision to rescind a timber sale and prohibit logging in eighteen thousand acres around the Medicine Wheel National Historic Landmark. The Forest Service had acted after developing a historic preservation plan for the Medicine Wheel, an eighty-foot-diameter rock circle with twenty-eight spokes of rock radiating from a central pile of stones. The Wheel, the most elaborate structure of its type in the West, was constructed long before Euro-Americans arrived and had historically been shared by the Arapaho, Cheyenne, Crow, and Shoshone tribes. The Forest Service held extensive consultations with groups of stakeholders, including historic preservation administrators, county officials, federal regulatory officials, and two Native groups with direct cultural affiliations with the site.[17]

The Mountain States Legal Foundation accused the Forest Service of violating its multiple-use mandate by developing a plan accommodating only the single mandate of the National Historical Preservation Act. Charging the Forest Service with promoting a religion by prohibiting logging in the area, the suit also said that in allowing Native groups too much influence, the agency had not fully accounted for the socioeconomic effects of the plan. Further, Wyoming Sawmills claimed to be offended by the religious symbolism of the Medicine Wheel.

The court disagreed with each of the plaintiff's points. It found that the socioeconomic considerations had been taken into account, and ruled that as long as the government is not advancing a religion, accommodating an Indian sacred site does not violate the Establishment Clause. The court also noted that although people have the capacity to be offended, a for-profit company does not. Furthermore, doing away with the plan would not remove the offending Medicine Wheel. Clearly, courts at the turn of the twenty-first century were beginning to treat Native religious sites with the same respect long afforded to Christian sacred sites.[18]

Although federal agencies were beginning to institute policies protecting Native Americans' use of sites sacred to them, and the courts were supporting those policies, such protection relied on agency "goodwill," and that was cause for concern.[19] In the case of Cave Rock this was not an issue. The Washoes fought what they viewed as the Forest Service's myopic vision regarding their concerns and the agency's inability to resist lobbying from the powerful Access Fund.

SEVEN

Common or Uncommon Ground

In the late 1990s the Access Fund found itself in what its leaders saw as a no-win situation. In the fund's 1997 online newsletter, Senior Policy Analyst Sam Davidson expressed concern that the rising incidence of conflicts between Indians and climbers at Cave Rock was damaging climbers' standing in the eyes of the public. He portrayed the climbers as beleaguered, saying: "Even our best and most compassionate efforts are causing our reputation to suffer." His "compassion" came into question in the following sentence when he termed the disputed properties "so-called 'sacred sites'" and went on to ask if there was anywhere climbing could be pursued where traditional Native Americans would *not* be offended. Should climbers abandon "every rock that Native Americans assert has spiritual value?" Regarding Cave Rock, which in the traditional Washoe view was a crossroads between the spiritual worlds above and below the earth, he wrote: "It's tough to be a force great enough to upset 'the equilibrium between earth and the spiritual realms.' "[1]

The next Access Fund newsletter featured protests from several climbers regarding Davidson's comments. "The claim that Native Americans are 'picking on' climbers since we are seen as a 'repressed and politically powerless' group is ludicrous," wrote one. Another agreed: "The Native American community has been so brutally raped that its few surviving members couldn't possibly represent a threat to the climbing community." Objecting to the Access Fund's defense of climbers' rights at Cave Rock, the writer continued, "This is not a question of legality. It is a question of ethics and respect." Another writer found Davidson's editorial snide and lacking in respect for the religious beliefs of Native Americans. Calling the piece "imperialistic garbage," the writer concluded: "I am totally appalled at the position you have taken on this issue and wish to be removed from your membership roster."[2]

Davidson responded, in the same newsletter, that he meant no disrespect to Native Americans. Climbers should support the efforts of Native people to revive their cultures, he said; but he wanted to see climbing values preserved as well. He feared a domino effect if climbers voluntarily agreed not to climb at sacred sites. Davidson cited the Devil's Tower/ Bear Lodge precedent, with its voluntary June closure, as a well-balanced and commendable solution to such problems and hoped it would be used as a basis for other negotiations.[3]

The chances of the Access Fund winning a similar resolution at Cave Rock rested with the man who would make the decision: Juan Palma, the newly appointed acting supervisor for the Forest Service's Lake Tahoe Basin Management Unit.[4] Palma had a degree in business management from Oregon State University and a master's degree in environmental sciences from the University of Nevada. At the time the Western Regional Office appointed Palma the acting supervisor for Lake Tahoe, his experience included stints as a budget officer, administrative officer, district ranger, and deputy forest supervisor.[5]

When Palma took up his post in spring 1997, climbing at Cave Rock was already a topic of conversation in distant venues. A May 18 article in the *Chicago Sun-Times,* for example, reflecting the Washoe perspective, commented: "The Washoe Indians, watching rock climbers crawl over one of their most sacred sites, wonder how the visitors would feel if teenagers slung ropes over the Western Wall [in Jerusalem] to practice rappelling. Or if rock climbers took to scaling the steeple of the National Cathedral. What if dirt bike racers rumbled each weekend through the Gettysburg battlefield?"[6]

When the previous supervisor, Robert Harris, had instituted the temporary climbing ban at Cave Rock, the Forest Service had received considerable public input—most of it from climbers. The Access Fund's strategy to eliminate the ban included mobilizing its constituents to overwhelm the decision makers with protests. The group had put out a call for responses, exhibiting sample letters online that its members might copy to send to the Lake Tahoe Basin Management Unit. The Access Fund had already appealed the closure to the Forest Service's Western Regional Office before Palma took his new position. The actions created pressure on the new Lake Tahoe supervisor to act quickly.[7]

Palma later said of the process involved in his decision making: "I deal with a lot of issues like [Cave Rock] every day of my life; it is part of what I do. . . . But actually, I enjoy it. I look at it like a big puzzle, and you can't quite find all the pieces. But, all of a sudden, you find a piece and it's a mystery how you found it." His attempt to put the Cave Rock puzzle together began on May 23, 1997. After the ban had been in effect for three months, Palma lifted it. The press represented the action as a win for climbers and the Access Fund. The *High Country News* of Colorado ran a headline that read, "Climbing Ban Fails." A *Tahoe Daily Tribune* front page heading announced: "Cave Rock Climbers Boosted by Lawyers: Legal Pressure Lifted Ban; Washoe Bitter." The long-term management plan for Cave Rock was scheduled to be announced six months later, in December 1997.[8]

In fact, two years would pass before even a preliminary decision was published. In August 1999 a Draft Environmental Impact Statement (DEIS) listing five management alternatives for consideration was issued, including Palma's preferred alternative. A public comment period would follow, leading to a Final Environmental Impact Statement and a final decision. Enmeshed in the bureaucratic process, the issue would remain unsettled for ten years after Palma's suspension of the ban. In 1997, though, presuming the policy would be finalized within a matter of months, Palma announced that in the meantime climbing would be permitted using existing fixed anchors. Setting new anchors was barred.

A Forest Service spokesperson revealed that Palma's decision resulted largely from lobbying by the Access Fund because government attorneys in the regional office felt the ban would be difficult to defend against some of the Access Fund's arguments. Washoe Tribal Chair Wallace said that tribal members felt a sense of betrayal. "The original decision gave them some hope," he said, "but now the elders are saying, 'Why should we have expected anything different?' "

Although he had lifted the ban, Palma encouraged climbers to continue to avoid the site out of respect for the Washoe people. He believed that the climbers would stay away once they learned about the Washoes' concerns. "What we really need is education," he said. Five days after the ruling, one seventeen-year-old climber said, "We went out there yesterday, and some of the best climbers in Tahoe were there. We're really happy just to be climbing back there again."[9]

Ten federal laws or policies were relevant in the case of Cave Rock. They ranged from the congressional acts protecting properties and regulating land use to those dealing with endangered species, sacred

Indian lands, and consultation with tribal governments. The Establishment Clause of the First Amendment was a primary concern. Time and again the prohibition against establishing a religion would be raised and weighed against the allowance of religious observance.[10]

Earlier in 1997, when Forest Supervisor Harris had instituted the ban, two local Tahoe climbers and Paul Minault, a San Francisco attorney who served as the Access Fund's northern California regional coordinator, met with Harris and asked him to lift it. When Harris refused, Minault appealed the decision to the Forest Service's Western Regional Office, arguing that the closure was unconstitutional because it eliminated a use of public land to accommodate the religious practices of a single interest group. Minault had prior experience in such land use issues because he had worked on the Devil's Tower/Bear Lodge case. That case, he contended, had established the precedent that the federal government cannot restrict public access because of Native American religious ceremonies.[11] These arguments formed the crux of the Access Fund's legal strategy throughout the decision-making process.

The Access Fund viewed the Devil's Tower/Bear Lodge decision as critical because the only loss it entailed to climbers was on a voluntary basis. The fund touted that decision repeatedly as an example of climbers' willingness to compromise and, owing to their 85 percent compliance in 1998, to observe a voluntary closure. Because the courts had consistently denied sacred land claims, the Access Fund also vigorously tried to tie Cave Rock to the Establishment Clause. Minault further claimed that the climbing ban did not meet the terms of the National Environmental Policy Act because it had not been preceded by studies of its environmental and social effects. He protested as well that Washoe Tribal Chair Wallace had been informed of the proposed closure and allowed to comment on it before it had been issued. That suggested bias in favor of the tribe and against climbers.[12]

Wallace pointed out that in revising the closure, the Forest Service had catered to individuals who live outside the Tahoe Basin while ignoring the needs of the Washoe people, who had been at Tahoe for thousands of years. "In their attempt to recognize the tribe's historical interest in Cave Rock," he observed, "the Forest Service ended up enshrining the rights of people who have been involved in its deterioration."[13]

Minault remained on the offensive, claiming that the tunnels and boat ramp had desecrated Cave Rock more than climbers had. "If they get rid of the cars and the boats and the sightseers, then fine, we'll go," he said. The Forest Service was hoping to avoid involvement in court disputes over the short-term closure and instead wanted to focus on a long-term solution that would "recognize the significance of Cave Rock."[14]

The Cave Rock dispute stalled when jurisdiction questions arose between Nevada agencies and the Forest Service. Chain-of-command issues surfaced as well because the site was in Nevada but the Lake Tahoe Basin Management Unit was administered in California, and its regional headquarters was in San Francisco. When he realized that the matter had bogged down, Wallace approached contacts in Washington, D.C.

A presidential summit that included President Clinton, Vice President Al Gore, and other top administration officials was set to be held at Lake Tahoe in July 1997. The conference would focus on environmental concerns regarding the lake. Wallace's lobbying got the Cave Rock issue placed on the agenda. The Washoes were encouraged when a suggestion arose at the summit that title to Cave Rock be assigned to the tribe. Repatriation of the site to the Washoe people was the one way to ensure its proper protection. A high-ranking Department of Agriculture official implied that the transfer would occur and assured the tribe members that they would be happy with the outcome of the matter. Nothing came of that assurance. There was no statutory means to transfer lands from the Forest Service to the tribe. Such a transfer would require congressional action.[15]

Wallace found an empathetic listener in Penny Rucks, the Forest Service's Heritage Resource Program manager for Lake Tahoe. Rucks had composed the documentation that qualified Cave Rock for the National Register, and it was she who, following the management unit's protocol, kept the tribe informed regarding Cave Rock's eligibility as a traditional cultural property and had sought Wallace's comments before the first climbing ban was announced.

The strategy of the Lake Tahoe Basin Management Unit for resolving the Cave Rock dispute began with public meetings to identify possible management practices for the property. Rucks had been scheduled to co-chair the meetings, but, discouraged with the government's handling of the issue, left the agency for another job before they began. Without Rucks, the sole authority for managing the meetings fell to Lisa O'Daly, an eleven-year employee of the Forest Service whose title was community planner. O'Daly now became the project manager for Cave Rock. To be decided was whether or not to restrict human activity at Cave Rock to protect its status as a National Register–eligible property, since ongoing activities, primarily climbing, might be having adverse effects on the integrity of the site.[16]

The Forest Service's attempt to broker a compromise by seeking concessions from both sides was doomed from the start. Wallace consistently stated that the tribe's sole concern was the integrity of the site, and that its importance could not be negotiated. The issue did not involve the number of climbers using the formation but the damage resulting from *any* unauthorized human presence.[17]

The Forest Service held the first collaborative meeting at the Zephyr Cove Resort, near Cave Rock, on the evening of January 22, 1998. Jan Cutts, an archaeologist from Inyo National Forest, served as the facilitator. Cutts was businesslike and authoritative as she kept the participants on track. The Forest Service had expected thirty-five to forty participants at the meeting, but the room overflowed with more than eighty people. The group was about equally divided between those who supported the Washoes and those in favor of climbing.

Jean McNichols, also known as Yetta, a descendent of Henry Rupert, spoke for the tribe. At the time, Yetta was acting as a caretaker for Cave Rock, going there periodically to offer prayers and to remove litter and debris. The Washoes did not want to be confrontational, she said, but they had to oppose any use of their spiritual site for recreation. Terry Lilienfield, a climber from South Lake Tahoe, spoke next. She stressed the climbers' respect for Cave Rock, agreeing that it is a powerful and spiritual place, and said that climbers wanted to find common ground with the Washoes.

The participants broke up into small discussion groups and then reassembled. Cutts and O'Daly kept the focus on individual feelings: why individuals were concerned and what their ideal Cave Rock would be. When participants expressed frustration, they were assured that future meetings would focus on solutions. The meeting met the goals of its organizers: to introduce the collaborative process and share the perspectives of the interest groups. Forest Supervisor Juan Palma, who would ultimately arbitrate the case, did not attend.[18]

Nor was Palma at the second collaborative meeting held two months later on March 10. This meeting featured John Maher, the Lake Tahoe Forest Service archaeologist. Maher explained Cave Rock's eligibility for inclusion on the National Register of Historic Places as a traditional cultural property and stated that rock climbing had been found to pose an ongoing adverse effect on the site's integrity. The criteria for an adverse effect included physical destruction, damage, or alteration of the property's character.[19]

This meeting also used small and large group discussions. The participants were asked to answer four questions:

1. What do I perceive the concerns about climbing at Cave Rock to be, and why?
2. What is special about Cave Rock to climbers, and why?
3. What activities other than climbing are a problem at Cave Rock, and why?

4a. [specifically for nonclimbers] What activities do you think the climbers are doing at Cave Rock?

4b. [specifically for non-Washoes] What do you think Cave Rock provides to the Washoes, and why are they concerned?

Some participants noted that only the second half of the last question dealt with Washoes while all the others dealt with climbers' issues and concerns.[20]

The meeting summary that was later mailed to the participants omitted Maher's assessment regarding the adverse effect of climbing on the site. Instead, Cutts reported on the large-group discussion, making the points that the climbers "are willing to do just about anything to retain access to the rock for climbing" and that climbers did not understand why they were being singled out when the Washoes believed that all non-Washoe presence at Cave Rock had a negative impact.[21]

On March 3, 1998, the climbers met by themselves and, "in an effort to show respect to and appreciation to those who revere the area differently than we do," proposed eleven things they would do differently while climbing at Cave Rock. These ranged from asking first ascenders to change their route names to placing signs in the area describing the site's significance to the Washoes, requesting respectful behavior and packing out personal waste, and replacing fixed slings with camouflaged equipment. Comparing Cave Rock with Devil's Tower/Bear Lodge, the climbers also offered to institute a voluntary closure during especially sacred periods or to leave when Washoes arrived and asked climbers to do so—provided that it happened "less than 6 times a year or so." The proposal continued, "Should tribe members begin to arrive on the site daily, asking climbers to leave, we would have to reconsider this agreement."[22]

Tribal Chairman Wallace responded that Devil's Tower/Bear Lodge was not a valid comparison. Many tribes shared that site, while the Washoes had a unique relationship with Cave Rock owing to its position as the center of their cosmology. Answering the criticism that only the climbers were attempting to compromise, Wallace said: "Washoes would respond that we've been doing that for the last 177 years."[23]

At the third collaborative meeting, held on March 17, the process nearly collapsed. One wall of the meeting room featured a large sheet of butcher paper. One end of the paper presented the climbers' ideal of free access to Cave Rock with no restrictions; the other end presented the Washoes' desire for complete closure to the public. Moderator Cutts stressed that the object of the meeting was to find middle ground where both sides could compromise. "What I'd like [you] to work on is somewhere between those two ends," Cutts announced. "We're trying to reach some place in the middle." She asked participants for their "thoughts on how Cave Rock can be used by everyone." The concept of compromise presented at this meeting clearly appeared to favor maintaining climbing at Cave Rock.

Juan Palma attended this meeting and addressed the group after Cutts' introduction. He spoke first of his childhood. "When I was a little boy about that high," he motioned with a hand, "my family and I used to spend almost every year [traveling]. We'd come from Texas, follow the crops, go up through California, up to Washington, and back to Texas." He told of riding in the back of a truck with others, "looking out the slats" and seeing forests and mountains, and wanting to live there when he grew up. He said he always knew he would end up in the mountains. He then spoke of his role in the process. He said he was willing "to make a decision anywhere along the continuum of options, including those that could affect the traditional cultural property." He too was seeking agreement, he said, and concluded with his hope that "we might be able to arrive at that point [of consensus] in the future, all of us together."[24]

Cutts then introduced Inyo National Forest Trail Program Coordinator Marty Hornick to explain basic climbing techniques and equipment to nonclimbers. Hornick, a climber, used a slide presentation and equipment demonstrations to brief the participants about climbing in general and climbing at Cave Rock specifically. Before he showed several slides of

Cave Rock he told the Washoes present that they could leave the room if they did not want to view the damage to the site. The photographs showed the tunnels, bolts, two-foot-long dangling slings, and the cave's paved floor.

At the conclusion of Hornick's presentation, which lasted thirty minutes, an audience member asked if the Washoes were going to present their perspective and if they would be given equal time. That was not on the agenda, Cutts said, but added that she would talk to the principals to see if something could be worked out.

During a break, as tribal members discussed whether or not to walk out of the meeting, the organizers decided that Tribal Chair Wallace could address the participants. Although given no time to prepare, Wallace spoke for twenty minutes. He thanked the participants for their contributions but explained that it was difficult for Washoe people to even discuss the site. He said that to the tribe, either a site is honored or it is not, and that it was unfair to ask them to compromise on their cultural values. A discussion followed. When participants were asked at the conclusion of the meeting if they thought another meeting would be a good idea, a show of hands revealed that a majority of the climbers but only one Washoe were willing to return. The summary of the meeting that Cutts sent to participants reported that "discussion topics from the participants included: It seems like the Washoe are not willing to even try to come to agreement, they will not settle for anything less than 'no presence' at Cave Rock; Climbers consider Cave Rock to be sacred to them—they have spiritual experience [*sic*] when climbing on it—why can't the Washoe accept the climber's connection to the rock?" The summary omitted the comments by Washoe tribal members and their supporters.[25]

The fourth collaborative meeting, on April 9, 1998, focused on brainstorming management options in small groups. Despite the vote at the last meeting, a number of Washoes attended. After ideas had been written and commented on, Terry Lilienfield spoke for the climbers, reiterating their position that they would like to work with the tribe to find solutions that would allow climbing to continue. Chairman Wallace restated the Washoes' appreciation for the opportunity to share ideas with the climbers and unwavering belief that Cave Rock's importance negated any possibility of compromise. He complained that tribe members were "depicted as uncompromising because they refused to agree to further destruction."[26]

The last meeting was held on May 27, 1998. Whether it was because people had grown tired of the process or did not believe it would accomplish anything, only two dozen members of the public were in attendance. Washoe elder Ruth Abbie spoke from the back of the room. Her voice was soft, and the room went still as everyone strained to listen. "The Great Spirit gave us this country. . . . We've tried to hang on to whatever we had. . . . We couldn't object to them destroying Cave Rock, this natural, pristine site. The government goes right in there and does what they want: build a road. That's progress. They never inquired of the Washoes. Do you understand how strongly the Washoes feel about that? When we try to fight for the little we have left, the sacred spots, well, it's just like talking in the wind."

Aaron Silverman, a climber from Reno, spoke in support of the Washoes' position. "For months and years now the Washoe have been telling people they don't want that piece of rock destroyed, and continually people are destroying it," he said. "We're now being given the chance to say [to them] this is your rock. . . . It seems to me that here in the Tahoe basin with as much rock as we have and as many areas as we have to climb in, why are we arguing. It's ridiculous arguing against these peoples' culture. C'mon; be real."[27]

Reno climber Rebecca Noyes, who seemed to speak for a number of members of the climbing community, challenged Silverman's perspective. Cave Rock, she said, is "one of the most beautiful places I've climbed in the world. And I've climbed throughout Europe and the United States. It is completely unique. One of the things that's so great about going through this process with the Washoe Tribe is to learn about how other people view Cave Rock and why it's important to them. And although I know they'd rather we didn't climb there, I can say that I climb there differently and I feel differently because of the things I've learned about the area. And it is that much more special because of that." While she understood that the tunnels had compromised the sacredness of the site, she added, she did not believe they had caused Cave Rock to lose its sanctity. "It just becomes more in need of special care," she said. "Sometimes we only appreciate things that are special to us when they are endangered, and I can certainly sympathize with that, while," she concluded, "I also like to climb there—very much."

Terry Lilienfield also disagreed with Silverman. Because of its world-class routes, she said, comparing Cave Rock with other Tahoe sites was comparing apples and oranges. She concurred with Noyes: "For myself, since I've leaned so much about the history of it, I do approach it much differently, and I do act differently while I'm there, but it hasn't diminished that I still want to be there."[28]

Perhaps addressing the complete lack of agreement between the two sides, Palma closed the meeting and the collaborative process by asking those in attendance to consider the question: "Have I lost myself in the process to [a point] where I am demeaned by it rather than [having] added to it?" Nonetheless, he concluded that he had enough information at that time to "lay out some alternatives for you and we will lay out the process. And if, in the end, we go to court that's okay; we go to court. But I hope that in the process we haven't lost friendships, but we have gained friendships."[29]

Another eight months passed before Palma announced his preferred alternative. Fifteen months went by before the agency published the DEIS and solicited comments from the public. Time merely ossified opinions. Palma would have to decide between their interests. There was no common ground.

EIGHT

Adverse Effects

When the participants were told they could leave at the conclusion of the last collaborative meeting, Cave Rock project manager Lisa O'Daly joked: "No! Lock the door. Make them talk." She had mentioned in the course of the meeting her hope that participants would come up with "a great solution" that would satisfy both the climbers and the Washoes. Climber Terry Lilienfield presented a more realistic appraisal: "We have tried to offer some gestures of respect . . . but we haven't found anything that is common ground. . . . It's not out of disrespect for the Washoe; Cave Rock is a really, really unique climbing resource as well. Climbers feel like we weren't there first, the Washoe were there long before us, but that doesn't diminish our love and respect for the area. . . . I wish we could get some sort of Washoe Peoples' blessing to climb there, but that's not going to happen."[1]

From the beginning of the controversy, some climbers had charged that the property lost its cultural significance when the first tunnel was blown through it. In part because of this allegation the Forest Service requested a formal determination by Carol Shull, the keeper of the National Register. In October 1998 Shull found that not only was its original eligibility as a traditional cultural property valid, Cave Rock also qualified as a historic transportation district and as an archaeological site. The geological study determined that the installations of fixed anchors for climbing affected the property's physical integrity, and Shull noted that some uses of the rock might be having adverse effects with regard to "setting, feel, and association of the historic districts."[2]

On learning of Shull's appraisal, Paul Minault wrote immediately to Forest Supervisor Palma to state the Access Fund's case. In a four-page letter he attempted to mitigate the determination's impact. Minault quoted Shull, the Tahoe Regional Planning Agency, and the Forest Service's own statements that while the rock had been desecrated by tunneling, tourism, and climbing, its importance to the Washoe tribe remained undiminished. In that case, he concluded, continued climbing would neither lessen the spiritual significance of the property to the Washoes nor reduce its historic integrity. He ignored the Washoes' claim that the climbers' presence diminished the site's spiritual significance and the finding that climbing posed an "ongoing, adverse effect."[3]

Minault attacked the Washoe tribe's "backward-looking" tactics, which he described as "demoniz[ing] climbers, inflat[ing] the significance of climbing impacts, and seek[ing] a prohibition on climbing at Cave Rock as a trophy of their resurgent political power." He urged Palma to take "a less intrusive management approach," allowing further time for the Washoes and others to build mutually beneficial relationships. Given time, he said, the groups might discover a commonality: "Climbers and the Washoe may find . . . that they share not only a reverence for Cave Rock, but an environmental viewpoint that is forward-looking and universalistic."[4]

Several months earlier Chairman Wallace had expressed offense at what he perceived as the climbers' attitude toward the Washoes: "The reaction that we have had to deal with and endure from a large part of the rock climbing community as to their presumptive interests or rights to [Cave Rock] is something that bothers a lot of tribal members who obviously have much deeper roots and a historical association to it." Wallace also disputed climbers' claims of reverence for the site and their contention that they looked on climbing there as a religious experience. He pointed out that the courts had not upheld the portrayal of rock climbing as having a religious basis or spiritual value. "That [climbing] is part of a larger cosmology, or that there is some metaphysical aspect to it, and being asked to equate that to the Washoe value and the significance of the site [to us] is a large leap of faith. That a recreational activity has taken on the proportions of a religion is something we don't accept."[5]

While one segment of the climbing community was claiming a spiritual or religious component to climbing, another faction was denouncing the Forest Service for becoming entangled in religion. In their view, "involvement of [National Historic Preservation Act] regulations at Cave Rock is just 'smoke and mirrors' behind which a religious purpose hides."[6]

Feelings continued to run high. Arguments included misinformation and were sometimes colored by racism. One climber wrote to the Forest Service: "Prior Washoe use (or non-use) of Cave Rock gives the tribe no legal right to impose their exclusionary demands on the American public. If they want to regain their tribal dignity and self-respect, let them take the massive tax credits and government support (that no other Americans enjoy) and create some honest jobs for their people."[7]

It was in this charged atmosphere that Juan Palma had to make his decision. Supporters of the tribe's position were cautiously optimistic. Two years earlier, in July 1997, when Palma was first appointed supervisor, the Forest Service had awarded thirty-year permits for tribal use of lands at Lake Tahoe's Meeks Creek Meadow and had granted the tribe the right to act as lessee of Meeks Bay Resort. The action, taken at the behest of President Clinton and Undersecretary of Agriculture Jim Lyons, ensued from the Lake Tahoe presidential summit. In being signatory to the accords, Palma had helped repatriate the Washoes to Lake Tahoe. In appreciation the tribe had issued a proclamation commemorating a special day in his honor.[8]

The fact that climbing had been found to pose an ongoing adverse effect at a site eligible for the National Register also seemed to point toward a decision favorable for the tribe. Climbing not only affected the historical integrity of the rock, it caused physical damage as well. Drilling into the rock to install bolts, for example, produced cracks that the freeze-thaw cycle opened even further. Palma had seemed to be leaning in the tribe's direction at the last public meeting when he said that he was unfazed by a possible court appeal; from the beginning the Access Fund had suggested it would litigate if Palma found in favor of the Washoe tribe.

On January 13, 1999, Palma issued his proposed decision. He explained that he had attempted to strike a balance between all those who consider Cave Rock important while protecting the site as a traditional cultural property. He deemed that "public access, including rock climbing, is allowed . . . and will be managed to minimize conflicts and impacts." Palma attached several stipulations to his proposal, among them no new routes, removal of routes that caused rockfall onto the road, removal of graffiti and the paved floor, and camouflaging the brightly colored slings. An important coda was that the site would be managed to reduce the effects of rock climbing that took place after 1996—the time Cave Rock was determined to be eligible for the National Register. Palma did not address the finding that activities of climbers diminished the setting, feel, and association of the traditional property, instead proposing that a reduction in climbing would mitigate its ongoing adverse effect on the site.[9]

Penny Rucks, the former Forest Service heritage resource manager, sent a scathing six-page response to Palma's decision. His proposed action would lead to further degradation of Cave Rock, she said, ultimately affecting its status as a traditional cultural property, and would bring into question the broader issue of the Forest Service's ability to manage such properties in accordance with historic values. She questioned an assertion that the proposed action "may affect" the historic property when the Forest Service had already determined that climbing "was an adverse effect." Had evidence to the contrary appeared? She asked that any finding that reversed or qualified the determination be sent to her.[10]

Rucks called Palma's proposal for a program "to inform people about the cultural and religious significance of Cave Rock" a "red herring." She reminded him that religious properties are ineligible for the National Register and asked, "Why persist in amplifying this confusion about religion and tradition?" Palma's choice to emphasize recreational use over the "rare and vital" example of Washoe culture, she argued, devalued the tribe's heritage. The decision's rationale "enhances the notion that Indian history and its monuments are somehow of less importance and due less respect than monuments of other historic events; it is in essence, I'm sorry to say, an ethnocentric, and discriminatory view."[11]

Rucks sent copies of the letter to the Regional Office of the Forest Service in San Francisco, the Nevada State historic preservation officer, and the primary federal policy adviser—the National Advisory Council on Historic Preservation—among others. The National Historic Preservation Act requires government agencies to consult with the appropriate state and federal preservation officials before taking action. The Council on Historic Preservation had not been formally consulted, although it had followed the issue since the original closure in 1996. After Rucks' letter, and other protests that followed, those organizations became actively involved in the process.

Rucks' letter showed how intently the procedure was being watched, and how closely it would be dissected. Agency justification for the decision was imperative. The DEIS presenting Palma's arguments as well as other alternatives was ready for distribution eight months later. On

August 17, 1999, Palma wrote to planning participants verifying his choice of the alternative allowing climbing.

Palma's letter introduced the 150-page draft impact statement. The document's abstract restated Palma's contention that his preferred alternative provided a compromise because "neither of the groups who most value Cave Rock get what they have expressed as their ideal conditions there."[12]

The DEIS presented five management alternatives for Cave Rock. The first called for no action, allowing all activities without regulation. The second, the one Palma favored, would allow public access while reducing climbing to the 1996 level. The third prohibited climbing and other recreation that physically affected the site. The fourth provided exclusive use to the Washoe. The fifth would manage the site consistent with the historic period prior to 1965—the year of the death of Henry Rupert, the last Washoe spiritual practitioner, whose association with Cave Rock contributed to its National Register eligibility.[13] Interested parties were given sixty days to respond, after which a final decision would be issued.

Project director Lisa O'Daly had coordinated the writing of the DEIS, which used information provided by eight Forest Service specialists on topics including heritage resources, recreation, geology, and wildlife. Chapter 1 of the DEIS explained the purpose and need for action at Cave Rock. Chapter 2 presented the alternatives, with O'Daly mounting a strong defense of Palma's decision in favor of alternative 2. She stated that the preferred alternative would allow public access while managing the property to reduce use of the site to that measured in 1996. The 1996 baseline grandfathered in sport climbing, which had begun at the site in the late 1980s. Viewed from that perspective, O'Daly wrote, the preferred alternative would not be authorizing activities that adversely affected the site but instead limiting them. This logic led to an amazing conclusion: "Thus, the undertaking actually positively affects heritage values rather than causing significant effects."[14]

Chapter 3, titled "Affected Environment and Environmental Consequences," carried the bulk of the argument to sustain Palma's decision. Its ninety-seven pages, which constituted approximately two-thirds of the document, discussed the proposed management direction. At one point in the chapter a long quote from Access Fund attorney Minault's 1998 letter to Palma bolstered the argument that although a determination had been made that climbing posed an ongoing adverse effect to Cave Rock's integrity, the feature nevertheless retained enough integrity to be eligible for the National Register. The document also quoted Minault's conclusion that "allowing climbing to continue would not reduce the historic integrity and spiritual significance of Cave Rock . . . at least provided that climbing was kept within its present limitations. In short, it is apparent that climbing has not significantly impaired the historical or cultural significance of Cave Rock, and consequently the protection of the historical and cultural significance of the formation does not require that climbing be prohibited now."[15]

The DEIS ended by noting that even if climbing did diminish the value of the property, it could be justified because the preferred alternative reflected "a condition of integrity" under the National Historic Preservation Act," which did not require preservation in every case.[16]

The DEIS also stated that removing some of the routes and camouflaging climbing equipment were steps toward restoration and rehabilitation, "albeit not to the level desired by the Washoe Tribe."[17] In fact, the only route removal the DEIS proposed was intended for the safety of the traffic on the roadway below, and camouflaging would be undertaken to reduce visual impacts, not to restore or rehabilitate the site.

Rucks' comment to Palma regarding religion as a "red herring" may have influenced the way O'Daly chose to discuss religion in the document, but it did not suppress the issue. Nearly two pages were given to the site's religious value to the Washoe.[18] After quoting the Establishment Clause of the First Amendment, O'Daly asserted that sacred and secular distinctions blur in many traditional cultures, and that discussing cultural values at a site in religious terms does not make the property less historically significant. She recognized President Clinton's Executive Order 13007 mandating that federal agencies avoid adversely affecting the physical integrity of sacred Indian sites, but then concluded her discussion with a rather sloppy presentation of the opposing view. "Conversely, some interested publics [*sic*] have alleged that recreation access restrictions to benefit a religious purpose violates Constitutional requirments [*sic*] regarding separation of church and state. They construe such measures as excessive government entanglement in religion."[19]

Basing her argument on the San Francisco Peaks case, which had allowed a ski resort to expand on land held sacred by the Hopis and Navajos, O'Daly implied that climbing was acceptable at Cave Rock because

Washoes were still permitted access: "The practitioners are free to worship through ceremonies and traditional rights and access to sacred sites is not prohibited by the Forest Service."[20] Although not discussed, this conclusion should not have been as easy to reach in 1999 as it had been in 1979. The acts of Congress and executive memorandums and orders issued in the interim mandated tribal consultation, protected Indian religious freedoms, prohibited damage to archaeological resources on Indian land, and clarified a federal-to-tribal government relationship.

Two other sections of chapter 3 emphasized that with the exception of paving the cave floor and putting graffiti on its walls, climbers had been acting legally in pursuing their activities. Several paragraphs in the "Social / Civil Rights Impact Analysis" section featured sympathetic comments about climbers, identifying them as environmentalists with "deep concerns for the land." O'Daly went even further and compared climbers' physical and emotional "intimate relationship" with Cave Rock to that of the Washoes, stating: "Both groups hold a deep regard for its striking presence." She quoted climbers and the director of the Access Fund in describing how climbing nourishes the spirit, and she spoke of climbers' "connection to the mountain" and "communion with vertical places." She placed confidence in the unwritten code of ethics that guides climbers. Regarding the question of whether climbers would follow regulations at Cave Rock with limited Forest Service enforcement, she concluded: "With the cooperation of the climbing community, and with knowledge regarding that community's code of ethics, the likelihood is high."[21]

Citations for the lengthy chapter included ten documents, five of which had been written by climbers or Access Fund officials. Three of the ten dealt with federal law as it related to sacred lands, and the other two were draft reports on Cave Rock. Although the draft reports included information on traditional Washoe use of the formation, conspicuously absent from the references was any material written by Native American specialists or the Washoes themselves.[22]

Palma's decision and O'Daly's document drew plaudits from climbers and expressions of bitter disappointment from the Washoes and their supporters.

NINE

Reactions

Juan Palma's decision and the release of the DEIS brought immediate responses; five letters arrived within the first two weeks. Three of the writers, one from the western slope of the Sierra and two from California's Central Valley, supported climbing. Their only objection to the proposal concerned the removal of the paved floor; all three suggested it be left in place. A husband and wife from Carson City, Nevada, wrote to ask Palma to reconsider and give maximum protection to the site. They worried that Native Americans might interpret his decision as denigrating their spiritual practices. The other letter came from the director of the Progressive Leadership Alliance of Nevada, an organization that represented thirty-six Nevada groups, including unions, women's groups, environmental groups, the ACLU, the Trial Lawyers Association, Citizen Alert, and the NAACP. The letter expressed the alliance's "extreme disappointment" in Palma's decision to allow the continued desecration of "this uniquely holy Washoe site" and asked him to amend it rather than allow the Washoes to experience "yet another profound injustice." Five of the six letters received in September 1999—two from North Lake Tahoe, two from South Lake Tahoe, and one from Idaho—supported climbing as well.[1]

Eight more letters arrived before the October deadline. Paul Minault, the Access Fund's attorney, wrote to urge Palma to remain steadfast in his decision, contending that the process had included all stakeholders and reflected "great integrity." Further, Minault stated that his group supported "voluntary" temporal restrictions on climbing that might allow Washoe practitioners to use the site. The other seven letters expressed support for the Washoes, and six were from notable entities urging Palma to revisit his decision. Robert Harris, who had held the position of forest supervisor now held by Palma, stated that the proposed alternative did not fully comply with laws protecting heritage resources and asked Palma how he could have selected an alternative that had significant environmental effects on a heritage resource.[2]

Washoe Chair Brian Wallace issued a lengthy rebuttal to the DEIS, which he argued, did not meet federal standards in addressing the adverse effects of climbing, did not sufficiently analyze potential adverse effects, and did not satisfy the requirements of the National Environmental Policy Act that reasonable alternatives not within the lead agency's jurisdiction be considered. This last, he remarked, could have meant considering an alternative that incorporated Washoe stewardship of the property. Wallace argued that Palma's decision to allow climbing at Cave Rock raised significant equal protection questions because it gave the tribe's historic and cultural site a lesser degree of protection than non-Washoe sites had received. He called the DEIS "a sad return to the way things used to be," and urged Forest Service officials to refer the matter to the Advisory Council on Historic Preservation as mandated by the National Historic Preservation Act.[3]

Forest Service officials did not have to look far to find the Advisory Council's opinion: the council had written after reviewing the DEIS. The council's letter said that the document did not appear to sufficiently balance site usage with the interests of historic preservation. Palma's preferred alternative weighed more toward protecting climbers' rights than protecting historic values. Further consultation with the tribe, the council, and the other agencies and users should continue to search for an alternative that better protected Cave Rock's historic values. The council also believed that the Establishment Clause concerns expressed in the DEIS were misplaced. A more protective alternative "would be secular," the council wrote, "providing for the management of federal land in a way that protects historic properties."[4]

A spokesperson for the Bureau of Land Management who had talked to Lisa O'Daly on the phone now wrote directly to O'Daly urging her to choose a different alternative: the one that would phase out climbing until all routes were removed and "lasting physical impacts were prohibited." The Nevada State Historic Preservation Office weighed in as well, saying that the Forest Service needed to more fully address the fact that climbing was having significant effects on a historic property. The chief of the Federal Activities Office of the Environmental Protection Agency, Region IX, assigned a "Lack of Objections" rating to the DEIS. But he too encouraged the Forest Service to continue consulting with the Washoe tribe "to ensure that the final decision is fully consistent with the Executive Order on Indian Sacred Sites."[5]

Wallace, the Advisory Council on Historic Preservation, and former supervisor Harris all recognized one paramount problem with the selection of Palma's preferred alternative: it did not follow the standards and guidelines of the Lake Tahoe Basin Management Unit's own forest plan. The plan's general management practice section included a priority listing of resources that was to be used in resolving conflicts.[6] The list ranked nine items in order of importance:

1. Protection of water quality in Lake Tahoe
2. Protection of threatened or endangered species
3. Preservation of significant cultural resources
4. Achievement of air quality standards
5. Maintenance of viable populations of wildlife
6. Achievement of diverse vegetation communities
7. Establishment of outdoor recreation facilities and uses
8. Harvesting and treatment of timber stands
9. Utilization of grazing forage

The list had been printed in the DEIS, but neither O'Daly nor the other writers had commented on it. Clearly Palma had disregarded the fact that the item mandating protection of cultural resources was third on the list and recreation was four places below it. Wallace called attention to the deviation from the forest plan, and the Advisory Council pointed out that the DEIS did not justify its divergence from the ranking system. Harris wrote that it was "of utmost importance" that the public be told why the forest plan was not followed.[7] Palma did not answer these objections.

Only one of those who responded to the DEIS seemed aware of the fact that Palma would not be making the final decision on an alternative. Climber spokesperson Terry Lilienfield closed her letter to Palma with the line, "Good luck in your new job, Lake Tahoe will miss you." Palma would be leaving the Tahoe area because he had taken a job as a Bureau of Land Management ranger in Oregon. His departure coincided with the issuance of the DEIS.[8]

Ed Gee, Palma's assistant, took over as acting supervisor for Lake Tahoe. He did little to pursue the Cave Rock issue, and the decision on the preferred alternative remained in limbo until May 8, 2000, when he attended a meeting with O'Daly; Minault and other climbers' representatives; Wallace; the Washoe tribe's general counsel, Tim Seward; tribal representatives; a consultant from the American Council of Historic Places; and a Department of Justice mediator. The mediator, who had prior experience negotiating many of the federal government's thorniest issues, led a frustrating day-long consultation that "failed to result in anything approximating agreement."[9]

Two months later the Advisory Council on Historic Preservation echoed the Bureau of Land Management's suggestion recommending that the Forest Service forgo its preferred alternative and select the alternative that phased out rock climbing at Cave Rock.[10] The Forest Service did not respond; a new forest supervisor was about to be named.

TEN

Record of Decision

Maribeth Gustafson, a nineteen-year career Forest Service employee, became supervisor of the Lake Tahoe Basin Management Unit in July 2000. She came to Tahoe after serving as the assistant director for fire and aviation management in the Pacific Southwest Region. After graduating from San Diego State in 1980, she had served as a resource officer, a district ranger, and an assistant forest supervisor. Her competence led many to wonder why she had not earned a forest supervisor position earlier. When Gustafson arrived at Lake Tahoe she visited Cave Rock with archaeologist John Maher—the same person who had taken Juan Palma to the site three years earlier to explain some of the intricacies of the issues. He gave Gustafson a similar presentation. Her reaction was quite different.

Gustafson began her decision-making process by personally reviewing everything that had been done on the issue: interviewing key participants, studying the DEIS and the public comments it generated, and watching videotaped recordings of the collaboration meetings. The principals involved in the dispute were not idle during this period. The Access Fund sought letters of support from its members and approached Congress. The Washoes turned to several Indian organizations for assistance, circulated an online petition, and raised the issue at the United Nations. Gustafson was struck by the vehemence of the opposing sides.[1]

In November 2000 another federal mandate was issued that affected the process. Executive Order 13175 directed government agencies to consult and coordinate with Indian tribal governments when making decisions that affected them. It was intended to strengthen federal government-to-tribal government relations. The order pointed out that tribes had been recognized as domestic dependent nations under federal protection since the formation of the United States. One section in the new directive stated that regulatory policies must be developed in consultation with tribal governments.[2]

That same year the section of the Code of Federal Regulations governing the Forest Service was amended to include a section entitled "Interaction with American Indian Tribes." The rewritten regulations required each agency's responsible official to "consult, invite, and provide opportunities" for tribes that might be affected by the planning process. It also required the responsible official to honor the government-to-government relationship.[3]

Gustafson had already been interacting with the Washoes' elected officials by listening to their claims and concerns. Following the requirements of the National Historic Preservation Act and the National Environmental Protection Act, she also met with traditional Washoe spiritual and cultural leaders who had relevant information regarding Cave Rock.[4]

At the same time, the federal government manifested a sudden, dramatic change in its approach to legal actions. The political leadership supportive of Indian causes under President Clinton had been replaced by pro-development advocates in the George W. Bush administration. The Washoes had cause for concern. In 2000, for example, Clinton's secretary of the interior, Bruce Babbitt, had denied a mining company's proposal to create a cyanide heap-leach gold mine containing three open pits up to 880 feet deep near Quechan Indian land on the border of Arizona and California. The area included a site of religious ceremonies and held ancient pottery shards and petroglyphs. In November 2001 Babbitt's successor, Gale Norton, overturned his decision and removed the protection from the sacred site. Norton was no stranger to western land-use controversies. In the early 1980s she had served as a senior attorney for the reactionary Mountain States Legal Foundation. Her chief counsel at the Interior Department had worked previously as a lobbyist for the American Mining Congress. Norton had not consulted with the Quechan tribe before reversing the policy.[5] Even as the Cave Rock protagonists maneuvered for an advantage, the Mountain States Legal Foundation and Wyoming Sawmills were instituting their court challenge to Forest Service policy regarding the Medicine Wheel National Historic Landmark, charging that protecting the Wheel promoted a particular religion.

Gustafson was not influenced by the sweeping changes in the federal perspective, or by the other legal challenges to the Forest Service. In early

2001 she completed her analysis of the Cave Rock situation and the probable effects of each of the alternatives proposed in the DEIS and submitted her report to the Nevada State Historic Preservation Office and the Advisory Council on Historic Preservation. Both supported the analysis. The council responded on March 21, 2001, urging her to select the alternative that offered the greatest protection to the historic values of the property. The council's response reinforced the idea that the qualities that gave Cave Rock its historic significance did not involve the First Amendment, and that protecting them would not endorse a religion. Rather, the council noted, "the primary purpose of prohibiting climbing would be to protect the integrity of a historic property."[6]

In June 2002 the Access Fund, its fears of a possible Cave Rock closure revived, escalated its lobbying campaign in Washington, D.C. The fund's policy director met with Nevada's representatives in Congress and with Senate officials as well as the House Subcommittee on Forests and Forest Health. Nevada senator John Ensign was receptive to the group's argument that the property should be "balanced" and managed for multiple use.[7]

The lobbying had no apparent effect on Gustafson. In October 2002 she issued the Final Environmental Impact Statement on Cave Rock (FEIS). Using parts of the five alternatives proposed in the DEIS she constructed a sixth, which she chose as the preferred action. Alternative 6 proposed eliminating climbing to provide maximum protection of the resource. The new proposal allowed other activities consistent with the historic period at Cave Rock, but that period was redefined as prehistoric times through 1965. The change from 1996, which the DEIS had used as the end of the historic period, to 1965 was the basis for prohibiting climbing.

The FEIS explained that Gustafson might have chosen any time period—the arrival of Euro-Americans at Cave Rock in 1848, the building of the Lincoln Highway, or a combination of periods—and then managed the site for the restoration or maintenance of those conditions. She selected 1965 because that was the year Henry Rupert died, and Rupert's association with the rock had contributed significantly to its National Register eligibility. His influence crossed cultural and ethnic boundaries as he adapted his healing practices to the changing world, exemplifying "the tension Native traditional practitioners maintain between tradition, experimentation, and innovation."[8]

The final Cave Rock decision had been pending for two years. When it appeared, it turned the temporary judgment upside down. The decision did not follow the example of the Devil's Tower/Bear Lodge agreement, which called for voluntary avoidance during significant periods. The new preferred alternative would manage Cave Rock to protect its status as a traditional cultural property, prohibiting any activity adversely affecting it. Gustafson dismissed the charge that religion was a factor in the proposal. "Some have characterized this issue as a Native American religion verses climber conflict, yet this is simply not the case," she said. "Rather the decision is actually based on resource values versus user impacts and ultimately, developed from solid resource priorities, and what I am charged to protect. The significant historic, cultural, and scientific values present at Cave Rock are deserving of maximum protection."[9]

The opposing sides now swapped offensive and defensive roles. The Washoes would defend the decision, as would the state and federal historic preservation groups. The Access Fund and climbing advocates attacked the ruling with every resource at their disposal. The chorus of protest was substantial. The Final Environmental Impact Statement was issued in October 2002. Senator Ensign requested a ninety-day extension of the usual thirty-day comment period. Ensign also contacted Mark Rey, the undersecretary for natural resources, and Forest Service Pacific Southwest Regional Forester Jack Blackwell to inquire why there had been such a radical change from the DEIS to the new alternative.

The Access Fund encouraged members to write not only to the Lake Tahoe Basin Management Unit but to Rey and Blackwell as well. The group provided mail and email addresses, phone numbers, and talking points. Despite Gustafson's statement to the contrary, the Access Fund encouraged its members to argue that the new alternative abrogated the Constitution by claiming religious preference for one group and would exclude legitimate public land users. Where three years earlier the DEIS had prompted 20 individuals or representatives of groups to write and comment, during the 120 days of comment for the final statement more than 1,400 responses were received.[10]

The comment period ended on March 31, 2003. Gustafson considered comments from both the draft and final impact statements. Four months later she issued the "Record of Decision." She chose alternative 6, banning climbing. In explaining her decision she noted the wide span of valid opinions regarding management of the site, commenting that she had considered them but did "not wish to debate them."[11] Nevertheless, in the "Record of Decision" she offered responses to a great number of the comments she had received during the comment period.

Many of those who had written in support of climbing had chosen the familiar theme that prior destruction from the tunnels and boating below the cave had already destroyed the value of Cave Rock as a cultural and historic site. To that point Gustafson responded that the Forest Service had no control over the highway or the lake. Because climbing caused adverse effects on Cave Rock, which did fall within the agency's jurisdiction, and since the property merited protection as a cultural site, the agency was working to limit damage as far as the supervisor's decision-making prerogatives allowed. To those who had urged a Devil's Tower/Bear Lodge–type compromise, Gustafson explained that unlike Devil's Tower/Bear Lodge, this decision was not made to accommodate religious practices. In an interview published in a local newspaper Gustafson explained that attempts to compromise had been made when Juan Palma was the forest supervisor and had been unsuccessful. It was time to act. "The situation has been handled by three forest supervisors. The first one took the same tack I'm taking."[12]

As might be expected—because the Access Fund chose to emphasize it—religion continued to be a common issue during the comment period, with writers approaching it from both sides. On the one hand, some claimed that "Cave Rock is sacred to climbers" and that climbing is a religious or spiritual activity. The supervisor responded that while the Forest Service appreciated the passion of the climbing community, "climbing does not meet the legal definition of a religion to receive the accommodation protections provided by the U.S. Constitution."[13]

On the other hand, many writers asserted that the ban on climbing promoted the Washoe religion, repeating a contention Lisa O'Daly had discussed in the DEIS: the National Historic Preservation Act was a subterfuge masking the religious reasons for the restrictions. Another comment stated that climbers did not interfere with the Washoes' spiritual use of the site. Gustafson replied that the law mandated the accommodation or use of sacred sites on public land, but because Washoe religious practices at Cave Rock were conducted in secret, it was difficult to ascertain how much climbing disrupted it. Regardless, Gustafson reemphasized her basic contention that "this decision is not a choice between religious use and recreation use; it is a decision to reduce impacts of recreational activities to an historic resource." She pointed out that the property's eligibility for the National Register of Historic Places was well documented; had been determined by the keeper of the National Register; and was supported by state, regional, and national resource professionals.[14]

A number of writers expressed concern that the right of the public to use public lands had been annulled and the democratic process denied. The supervisor replied that if "democratic" meant being put to a vote, the statement was correct. Agency decisions were made by managers, not by a particular group or the general public. On the other hand, the extensive public participation in the process had been consistent with federal law, and the public's right to participate had been honored. When thorough consultation with resource professionals and vested interests had failed to resolve the conflict, the supervisor made her decision by following the Forest Service Management Plan. She referred to the plan's hierarchy for resolving conflicts that Supervisor Palma had disregarded, pointing out that "preservation of cultural resources" is ranked third in importance while "establishing recreation facilities" is seventh.[15]

To the contention that the agency's decision unfairly restricted the rights of a group of users, the supervisor responded that the Forest Service has a duty to ensure fair use of federal land. But "a 'fair share' of the [Lake Tahoe] basin capacity does not require the agency to allow every activity everywhere." She then listed analogous examples at Lake Tahoe, including restricting fires in the wilderness to protect its setting and prohibiting grazing in watersheds to protect water quality. One of those who commented had envisioned a "slippery slope" if traditional cultural properties could be used to restrict climbing or other activities. To that Gustafson replied that further restrictions were indeed possible because properties of significance are valid resources worthy of protection.[16]

ELEVEN

New Directions

The Forest Service would not begin implementing the new management direction until forty-five days plus five working days after the decision was published in the local newspaper. Implementation would be postponed if the decision came under administrative appeal during that period. Two appeals were filed within that time frame—one by the Access Fund, the other by climber Terry Lilienfield—and so the climbing ban did not go into effect. The decision was rendered on July 8, 2003, and the Final Environmental Impact Statement signed on August 5. The appeals were filed with the Forest Service Pacific Southwest Regional Office in September. They would first be considered by an appeal reviewing officer and then sent for final dispensation to the regional forester. On November 5, 2003, Deputy Regional Forester Kent P. Connaughton affirmed Forest Supervisor Gustafson's decision. The appeal reviewing officer had reported that the Cave Rock decision was appropriate in that "all laws, policies, and regulations were followed." Connaughton commented on each issue raised by the appellants and found that each was addressed adequately in the impact statement and "Record of Decision."[1]

Lilienfield said she was disappointed by that decision because she felt that climbers were being singled out, but she would not continue the fight. The Access Fund was another matter. Attorney Paul Minault protested that the Forest Service's multiuse mandate is meant to ensure balanced usage of federal lands. "I can't think of any precedent for this," he said. "It seems to us if the Forest Service is really sincere in resolving the conflict, it would find a middle ground." He contended that the dispute had nearly been resolved when Juan Palma was the forest supervisor. The tack of portraying Gustafson as a new supervisor who entered the process halfway through and was unwilling to find a compromise solution would become part of the case the Access Fund presented to the public.[2]

In December 2003 Steve Matuse, the Access Fund's executive director, announced that the organization had filed a federal lawsuit challenging the ban. He told the *Tahoe Daily Tribune* that "the Access Fund at one time had an acceptable plan worked out with the forest supervisor who preceded Gustafson." A "Cave Rock Q & A" section on the fund's Website posed the question: "Who was involved in making that decision and how did the planning process occur?" The answer first mistakenly said that the "acknowledged traditional Washoe belief" held that Cave Rock should be "avoided by all people except for only a few male Washoe religious practitioners." The Website then portrayed Gustafson's actions as unwarranted supervening. After three years under the preferred alternative 2, which allowed limited climbing, the fund charged, "a new forest supervisor, Maribeth Gustafson, abruptly reversed the previous management direction at Cave Rock by unexpectedly introducing a completely new Alternative 6 . . . and thus essentially rejected the years of hard work and consultation with the various interested parties."[3]

The Access Fund had changed its public relations strategy after the 1997 Davidson editorial debacle, which had presented disparaging remarks about sacred sites. As in all Access Fund postings regarding Cave Rock since, Matuse stressed that the organization's complaint involved the Forest Service, not the Washoe tribe. The Access Fund routinely negotiated with Native groups to resolve conflicts, he said, giving the example of one of their directors who had traveled to northern California to meet with tribal representatives over a burial site issue the week before. Matuse commented that the Cave Rock situation was more complicated because the Washoes "have never spoken to us and refuse to speak to us."[4]

At the filing of the Access Fund's lawsuit, the Forest Service again agreed to postpone implementation of the ban. It was not until January 28, 2005, a year and a half after Gustafson announced her decision, that the case came before District Court Judge Howard McKibben in Reno. Observers found it difficult to speculate how McKibben might view it based on his previous decisions. His rulings followed legal precedents and statutory provisions, but he did not issue written records explaining his findings. In several suits filed by Native Americans he had supported government entities over tribal interests.

In a highly publicized case in 1993, for example, McKibben issued a nine-month jail sentence to an elderly Western Shoshone man found guilty of assaulting a federal officer. The man had doused himself with gasoline and threatened to ignite a lighter if federal officers did not release the 269 horses they had captured in a raid near the man's ranch. The assault charge came after Bureau of Land Management agents wrestled the man to the ground to make sure that he would not carry out his threat. In 2002 McKibben had allowed a government sale of Shoshone cattle confiscated on land claimed by both the BLM and the tribe. The following year the Paiute tribe and the government together sought judicial review of a McKibben ruling that had affirmed a Nevada state engineer's decision favoring landowners' water rights over those of the Paiutes at their Pyramid Lake Reservation. In that instance the Ninth Circuit Court affirmed part of McKibben's ruling, reversed part, and remanded part for rehearing.[5]

A McKibben case from 2004 also seemed to shed some light on his judicial temperament regarding Native antiquities. He sentenced two men to relatively short sentences—two months and four months, respectively—after they were convicted of stealing large boulders covered with one-thousand-year-old petroglyphs for their personal use in landscaping.[6] The questions raised by McKibben's rulings and the fact that in the Cave Rock case the government was charged with violating the First Amendment while protecting an Indian site kept the litigants on both sides guessing as to their chances.

A team of attorneys headed by Laurence K. Gustafson (ironically, the same last name as the forest supervisor) from Dallas, Texas, argued the case for the Access Fund. Attorney Gustafson specialized in the defense of corporations and their employees in antitrust and environmental litigation as well as corporate criminal proceedings. The crux of the suit now brought against the Department of Agriculture, its secretary, and the Forest Service was similar to the earlier appeal: the Establishment Clause of the First Amendment had been violated. The Access Fund also contended that Gustafson had unexpectedly and unjustifiably reversed direction, acting arbitrarily and capriciously under the Administrative Procedure Act, the federal law that governs the way agencies may propose and establish regulations.

McKibben listened to the arguments and questioned the attorneys. He then followed his usual procedure, making his decision from the bench that same day without issuing a written record. Although he might not necessarily have made the same decision the forest supervisor had made, he said, he rejected the Access Fund's arguments. Since the supervisor had observed all applicable laws and followed her agency's policies, he found no reason to annul her decision. He found in favor of the Forest Service with regard to the Access Fund's contentions concerning the First Amendment and Supervisor Gustafson's actions under the Administrative Procedure Act, and he upheld the climbing ban.[7]

McKibben's decision did nothing to change the principals' opinions. Tribal attorney Tim Seward said the ruling finally accorded tribal cultural resources the same level of legal consideration other national resources received. A climber complained that a "privileged and politically powerful minority" had been allowed to impose its will on the "public at large." Minault continued to contend that the closure was a religious determination, and that the tribe had received special consideration: "We think the Forest Service just rolled over by treating public property like private property, and giving the Tribe the taboo closure they want." Supervisor Gustafson commented that an effective management strategy could finally be put into effect to protect an important landmark.[8]

Gustafson's statement was optimistic. The Access Fund's directors were worried that hundreds of public land units might be similarly affected if the organization allowed a legal precedent to be established. On March 22, 2005, calling the ban "unreasonable and unnecessary," the Access Fund announced that it would appeal the decision to the Ninth Circuit Court of Appeals.[9]

The court heard the case on February 15, 2007, in San Francisco. Each side was allowed fifteen minutes of oral arguments, after which the judges questioned the attorneys. Because the appeals court would decide only whether the district court had made a legal error, no new arguments were allowed. The Access Fund's legal team, still headed by Laurence Gustafson, pursued the by now familiar complaints that the Establishment Clause had been violated and the Forest Service's action was arbitrary and capricious.

Specifically, the appeals court had to determine if the lower court made a mistake in interpreting the applicable phrase in the First Amendment of the Constitution: "Congress shall make no law respecting an establishment of religion, or prohibiting the free exercise thereof." In 1984 the Supreme Court had determined that complete separation of church and state is unnecessary, and that in fact, all religions must be afforded not merely tolerance but accommodation.[10]

Lemon v. Kurtzman (1971), which prohibited allocating federal money for religious schools, served as the court's benchmark. That case produced "the *Lemon* test"—three questions to determine whether an action violates the Establishment Clause: (1) Does the case have no secular purpose? (2) Is the principal effect of the case to promote a religion? (3) Does the case involve excessive entanglement with religion? If any of the three questions is answered in the affirmative, the action is unconstitutional. Conservative Supreme Court justices have criticized the *Lemon* test, resulting in a patchwork pattern of enforcement. Some circuit courts use it and some do not. The Ninth Circuit panel noted that although not "sanctified" by the Supreme Court, the *Lemon* test had not been overruled and so continued to serve as the best analysis tool available.[11]

The Access Fund's suit declared that the Washoe tribe's consistent reference to Cave Rock as a religious site violated the first question. The group also charged that the Forest Service had labeled the site a cultural property merely to evade legal challenges. "Listing Cave Rock as a traditional cultural property does not change the fundamental nature of Cave Rock as a religious site," the complaint argued.[12]

The court disagreed, noting that the Forest Service had consistently stated, and presented thorough documentation, that a secular purpose motivated the protection of Cave Rock as a cultural, historical, and archaeological monument. The agency had decided that although the property might at times be discussed in religious terms, its significance was not based on Washoe religious doctrine but on the historic and ethnographic record. Quoting a previous finding by the Tenth Circuit Court that recognized "the historical, social, and cultural significance of religion in our lives," the Ninth Circuit Court of Appeals decision stated that a site's religious significance does not disqualify it as a national monument. In fact, the court provided examples of religious sites that *are* national monuments, including the National Cathedral in Washington, D.C.; the Touro Synagogue, the oldest remaining synagogue in America, dedicated in 1763; and the Sixteenth Street Baptist Church in Birmingham, Alabama, which played a pivotal role in the Civil Rights movement. The court concluded that the property's secular value having been established, "the fact that Cave rock is a sacred site to the Washoe does not diminish its importance as a national cultural resource."

The Access Fund's complaint had included comparisons of Cave Rock with Devil's Tower/Bear Lodge and with National Arch and Bridge in

Utah, where usage conflicts had been solved with voluntary closures. Once the court determined that the Cave Rock ban was for secular reasons, those comparisons were dismissed, because in the other two cases the voluntary closures were advanced for solely religious goals. As an aside, the court noted that in the case of Devil's Tower/Bear Lodge, climbing had been shown to be a legitimate historic use of the land dating back to the late 1800s.

Regarding the second prong of the *Lemon* test, the Access Fund argued that the government's actions showed a preference for the Washoe religion over others. The court noted that in addressing that issue, the judiciary often looked to the character and purposes of the group that is benefited. Because the Washoe tribe favored an alternative that precluded all activities at the site except those it sanctioned, and the Forest Service alternative provided for public use activities inconsistent and incompatible with Washoe beliefs, the court viewed the action as permissible accommodation rather than impermissible endorsement. The court found no evidence that the Forest Service was acting to advance the Washoe religion. There was no hint that the agency favored tribal religion over other religions or that the decision implied disapproval of the religion(s) of Access Fund members. "The facts reflect only that the Access Fund's members, whatever their religious beliefs, would prefer to continue climbing on the rock, and the government's policy prevents them from doing so."[13]

Access Fund lawyers claimed that the Forest Service ruling violated the third *Lemon* test question as well by entangling the government in religion. In limiting free access to Cave Rock, they said, the ban would "coerce the public . . . to support [Washoe religious] interests." In this view the ban would lead to the proscribed intertwining because the Forest Service would have to police it. The court responded that monitoring recreation activities would be no different from monitoring visitors dumping trash. The court held that the Forest Service had acted within the law on all three *Lemon* tests, and so had not violated the Establishment Clause.

The Access Fund's last hope to overthrow the decision lay with its claim that by discriminating between climbers and other recreational groups Supervisor Gustafson was acting in an arbitrary manner, and that her reversal of Palma's decision had been capricious. Climbing activities, the Access Fund said, had caused no significant geological damage that would call for a ban. The court replied that the last argument "misse[d] the point" because the value of Cave Rock is cultural and historical as well as geological. Further, climbing harms the physical, not necessarily the geological, integrity of the rock. The court concluded that the ban, "adopted after deliberate and thoughtful analysis and based on nonarbitrary historical considerations, does not violate the Administrative Procedure Act."[14]

The final ruling was not filed for six months. On August 27, 2007, more than four years after the Forest Service's final decision was announced, the court had upheld that pronouncement. The court's opinion had been written by Circuit Judge M. Margaret McKeown and affirmed by Judge J. Clifford Wallace. Judge Wallace wrote separately citing the question of the "continuing validity" of the Lemon test, which, he said, was not applicable when analyzing the claim under the Establishment Clause. Instead, he used a 2005 Supreme Court decision, *Van Orden v. Perry,* and came to the same conclusion. *Van Orden* upheld the ruling that the placement of a Ten Commandments monument on the Texas State Capitol grounds did not violate the Establishment Clause. That case looked toward "the strong role played by religion and religious traditions throughout our Nation's history." As had been the case in that finding, Judge Wallace saw a dual significance in the climbing ban. "Although it may promote Washoe religion," he wrote, "it also protects a culturally, historically, and archaeologically significant site." He therefore found that the Forest Service had acted legally.[15]

The Forest Service's own formal review, a district court decision, and a circuit court finding—which used two different criteria—had rejected the Access Fund's arguments. With the last decision, the climbing group gave up its legal challenge.

Climbers had lost a valued resource; the Washoes had regained one.

TWELVE

Connections

The steep trail up to Cave Rock levels out at a switchback and leads either into the cave or across the cave apron to a small stone patio overlooking the vast expanse of Lake Tahoe. A mid-February 2009 visit revealed that the graffiti, the paved floor, and the anchors in the rock remained. Several names and dates, timeworn but obtrusive, were inscribed on the walls. A Forest Service sign reading "No installing of rock climbing hardware" leaned against a wall. Overhead, where the rock opens and rises to fifty feet and then continues up another one hundred feet, abandoned bolts, carabineers, and slings still marked phantom routes.

Half a dozen large natural rock benches lined the main portion of the cave. Short, narrow, pea gravel paths led around a circle of slightly larger, irregular rocks to another granite mosaic floor. Beyond the floor, uneven ground inclined to the cave's dark back wall. In front of the floor, smoke from a recent fire blackened one wall and the overhanging roof. A couple of cobbles broken from the flooring were positioned as part of the fire ring. A branch of sage on the ground nearby might have been evidence of a Washoe practitioner's recent visit. Except for an occasional vehicle rushing through the tunnel below, the site was silent.

A year earlier, on February 26, 2008, the climbing closure had become permanent. Forest Order 19-08-01 allows noninvasive recreational activities but manages the site for its historical and archaeological significance. The agency was waiting for funding to remove the climbing artifacts and graffiti.

None of the most visible principals in the conflict were actively engaged in it by the time the climbing ban became final. After the district court judgment in 2005 upheld her decision, Maribeth Gustafson became the forest supervisor of the White River National Forest in Colorado.

In 2008 she was promoted to the position of deputy regional forester in Denver. Former supervisor Juan Palma continued to find administrative positions in other government organizations. Lisa O'Daly left the Forest Service to become a planner for the city of South Lake Tahoe. Brian Wallace lost a reelection bid in 2006 after serving as Washoe tribal chair for sixteen years. He is a political consultant on Native affairs, and in 2008 served on the National Native American Advisory Council for Bill Richardson's presidential campaign. Local climber Terry Lilienfield stopped climbing at Cave Rock years before the last court finding. Access Fund Policy Analyst Sam Davidson and Regional Representative Paul Minault retired from their positions, and the fund no longer mentions Cave Rock in its publications.

The importance of the Cave Rock issue is irrefutable. After the district court decided in favor of the Washoes, Tribal Chair Wallace commented: "Many of us waited our entire lives for a moment like today." Forest Service archaeologist John Maher concurred, saying it was "a once in a lifetime case."[1]

The legal framework necessary to make the Cave Rock determination had its roots in public awareness of Native peoples' causes raised in the 1960s and 1970s. Indian activism, growing academic recognition, and lobbying created an atmosphere for action by the federal government's executive and legislative branches. Those acts, toothless with regard to enforcement, led the Forest Service—an agency with the power to implement an enforcement mechanism—to find in favor of recognizing and restricting damage to the property.

The decision sustains the theory that agency management, in conjunction with statutory provisions and enforcement by the judiciary, is a viable form of protection for sacred sites. In the case of Cave Rock, the administrative agency's personnel were closer to the issue and the contesting parties than were the judges or lawmakers. Although compromise was ultimately found to be unworkable, agency officials were able to fully explore possible concessions. Officials considered the role of religious values in a way that courts, because of strict precedents regarding property or liability, could not. And the narrower, site-specific decision was easier to uphold in the appeals process.[2]

But the Cave Rock dispute was very nearly decided in opposite fashion. Two forest supervisors, Juan Palma and Maribeth Gustafson, viewed largely the same evidence, came to different conclusions, and made radically different decisions. Palma sought to find a middle ground that would mollify both sides. He never seemed to grasp the depth of the Washoe tribe's antipathy toward a compromise that in their view would continue to desecrate the property. Gustafson recognized early in her analysis the cultural importance of Cave Rock, not only to the tribe but to the public as well. "Having determined that Cave Rock was a valid historic and cultural resource for which I was responsible and should protect," she said, "I viewed this as a conflict between resource values and user impacts." She then applied the Lake Tahoe Basin Management Unit Forest Plan's direction for resolving resource conflicts, and the preservation of cultural resources outweighed recreation.[3]

Gustafson's emphasis on the site's cultural and historical importance rather than its religious significance may have been the primary factor in the court's decision to uphold her determination.[4] If the Cave Rock decision had been based on the religious qualities of the site, in all probability the courts would have been unwilling to mandate its protection. This is why the Access Fund attempted at every opportunity to portray the issue as religious promotion versus public access.

Fortunately for the Washoe tribe, Cave Rock's cultural and archaeological significance were evident. The site's status as a historic transportation district was important too. Because its properties were of national interest, the site qualified for the National Register as a traditional cultural property. While acknowledging that the Washoes spoke of Cave Rock in religious terms, Supervisor Gustafson stressed the importance of its historical significance and heritage value. In doing so she circumvented the climbers' claim that the government was promoting religion.

The Access Fund felt compelled to challenge the district court's finding because the decision had national significance. "Not doing so," one of its spokespersons noted, "could create a legal precedent leading to future unreasonable and unnecessary closures of public lands."[5]

The case of Cave Rock does have national implications. It is the first time a climbing site has been involuntarily closed out of respect for Native culture. It shows that when correctly pursued, there are laws in place that will protect Native people's traditional properties. At the same time, the site has unique qualities and so may not be as precedent setting as sacred site advocates wish and climbing activists fear. Mitigation measures that were inadequate at Cave Rock may be appropriate elsewhere. The policies, orders, and laws provided by Congress and the executive branch had to be employed along with the Lake Tahoe Basin Management Unit Forest Plan's priorities to protect the resource. This mutual action left the courts no alternative but to uphold the decision.

Allowing continued public access to Cave Rock gave evidence that the determination to ban climbing was not done to promote religion. In their attempt to maintain the correlation between shamanism and health, the Washoes had argued for the prohibition of all non-Washoe activity at the rock. The fact that the decision violates a core tenet of their beliefs proved that the action was not an impermissible government endorsement. In any case, for the Washoes, the imperfect finding ended the impact and damage of climbing. The tunnels and the boat ramp below the cave remain, and Washoe practitioners still confront problems similar to those experienced by Henry Rupert. The Washoes' connection to the site, a preeminent symbol of the relationship between humans and nature, has been maintained. To them, Cave Rock, dominating Lake Tahoe's eastern shore, continues to evoke its spiritual power.

Afterword

The Cave Rock DEIS, published in 1999, suggested that the Forest Service might not be able to find anyone willing to remove the metal anchors from the rock face because it would require specialized skills found exclusively in the climbing community. The section summarizing social effects said: "Members of that community may be reluctant to be hired on for such a controversial task."[1] The DEIS writer had not considered the fact that there were many climbers who had honored Washoe wishes and refused to climb at the site. Presumably a number of those would want the face returned to a boltless state.

In spring 2009, with the infusion of funds from the American Recovery and Reinvestment Act, the Forest Service sought a contractor to clean up Cave Rock. Besides athleticism and the ability to climb, whoever undertook the task would need a particular set of skills including experience working at great heights, a knowledge of hand tools, the mechanical expertise to create safety and rope-and-pulley systems, and an innovative bent that would allow adaptation when new sections created problems such as extreme overhang, difficult angles, or long distances between anchors.

John Dayberry, an educator and conservationist with a California contractor's license, talked to Darrel Cruz, the cultural preservation officer for the Washoe tribe, and, believing he could do the job, submitted a bid to the Forest Service. Dayberry had worked for the tribe in the late 1990s as an engineer—among other tasks helping to restore Meeks Creek at Meeks Bay. He had followed the Cave Rock controversy for years, all that time thinking that perhaps he might be the one to restore the site. An avid skier, he had forsaken climbing some years earlier after losing the tips of two fingers while working as a mechanic on ski lift towers at a local ski resort. Dayberry undertook the job in the spring of 2009. It would be the most difficult and challenging work of his life.

On May 3, 2009, a *San Francisco Chronicle* headline announced "Crews Remove Climbing Bolts from Tahoe Landmark." Although others would assist in the work of erasing graffiti and removing the cement and imported rock from the cave floor, the crew that removed the bolts consisted only of Dayberry and Bill Atkins, a friend who had formerly worked on large environmental cleanup and restoration projects. While Atkins belayed from above, Dayberry dangled on a climber's rope, working on the rock face. Removing the anchors required overcoming technical problems. Not only did he have to remove the bolts, the metal sleeve that contained each bolt had to come out as well, and the holes then needed to be filled with native rock that would remain in place.

Dayberry discarded a suggestion that he mix crushed native rock and epoxy to stuff into the holes, envisioning epoxy running down his arm while he was working on holes in the overhang. Instead he utilized a method, suggested by his wife, Jodi, prefabricating plugs using sheets of native rock collected from road construction debris. Using a drill press, his son Trey punched out ⅜-inch plugs that Dayberry carried to the rock face and glued in place using a calking adhesive.[2]

Dayberry began on Kona Wall, below the highway. Its overhang was less dramatic than the Lower Cave and Main Cave routes, making it an easier place to work. There, Dayberry could perfect the basic techniques he would utilize throughout the project. Wearing a climbing harness and sitting on a bosun's chair, a five-gallon bucket of tools hanging from his belt, he descended on a static line. Once experimentation showed which tools worked best for which circumstance, the work on Kona Wall preceded in relatively smooth fashion.

When Dayberry moved to Lower Cave, below the road, he had to confront the problems associated with working on the underside of overhanging rock faces. To pull himself against the face he used a cheat stick and extension that could reach as far as twenty feet. A carabineer on the end of the stick could be snapped onto another in the rock, enabling Dayberry to pull himself close. Problems with using the cheat stick in the wind while the bosun's chair twirled caused long delays. He suspended bolt removal altogether on particularly windy days.

When he worked in the main cave area above the highway, it took him an hour and a half to set up each morning. Pitons, anchors, and cams were set on the very top of the feature to secure the ropes, and then Dayberry would be lowered one hundred feet or so to dangle near the largest concentration of bolts. The most difficult bolts to remove were in the 5.13 and above routes, where he needed to pull himself up and in to work while hanging.

He also had to take out anchors set on the upper reaches of the rock's face, working eyeball-to-eyeball with seagulls, hawks, and, one memorable day, a bald eagle. It had been suggested that those holes might be left unplugged. Dayberry knew that they had to be filled because early masons had used similar holes to allow ice to crack and break rock along just such lines.

Perhaps the most dangerous aspect of the job involved the fall when moving from one bolt placement to the next. After securing himself to a set anchor, Dayberry jammed a temporary cam or nut into a crevice and moved the rope from the anchor to the temporary device. After removing the bolt and sleeve and plugging and cementing the hole, he held himself with a hand jam, removed the cam, and let go. The fall could be up to twelve feet depending on the location of the next bolt. Each fall jarred Dayberry, his tools bouncing wildly in the bucket, and swung him into the eight-millimeter rope that secured his next station. Another hazard was the belay rope fraying as it dragged across sharp granite edges. When asked about it, Dayberry shrugged and said, "That's why I had backup rope."

Other dangers involved the instability of the rock. Once, immediately after unhooking from a rock and falling to his next site, a piece broke off, crashing against Dayberry's hardhat and glancing off his shoulder. Another time the place where he had been working the previous afternoon looked different when he arrived the following morning. It took him a minute to realize that a four-hundred-pound boulder had broken free and fallen to the cave floor. Had it broken free while he was working, it would have taken him with it. On a third occasion Dayberry dislodged a sixty-pound rock while being lowered to a work site. The rock fell past the cave floor and hit against the horse fence put up alongside the highway in case of such an eventuality. The fence stopped the rock just as a Toyota sedan emerged from the tunnel directly in its path.

It took a six-person crew four and a half days to break up and remove the flooring from the main cave. A generator-powered jackhammer, its electrical cord running 120 feet down to the road, loosened the mortar. The operator took care not to work into the original rock and dirt beneath the flagstone. The thirteen thousand pounds of debris removed during the operation comprised four yards of imported rock and cement and two yards of pea gravel.[3] Forest Service archaeologist John Maher made periodic inspections during Dayberry's work. On the day of the floor removal, tribe member Ed James also examined the site to be certain no artifacts were in the debris.

The final task was removing the graffiti from the walls. When Dayberry and his crew finished, the cave looked much as it had when Henry Rupert had used it.

Dayberry is confident that many in the climbing community approve of what he did. "Since doing the work, 80 percent of the climbers I've encountered are happy for the tribe. . . . Most feel it's the least we could do for them." He came away from the work more certain than ever that it needed to be done. Flaking of rock on the site's face had destabilized many of the bolts, and he found water behind bolts in the cave ceiling. Sooner or later all of them would have failed. Ultimately, they were unsustainable.

NOTES

INTRODUCTION

1. Robert F. Heizer and Albert B. Elsasser, "Some Archaeological Sites and Cultures of the Central Sierra Nevada," *Reports of the University of California Archaeological Survey* 21 (Berkeley: University of California, 1953), 9; Andrew Todhunter, *Fall of the Phantom Lord* (New York: Doubleday, 1998), 29.

2. Jones and Stokes Associates, Inc., *Cave Rock Management Plan Final Environmental Impact Statement* [hereafter FEIS] (Sacramento, Calif.: Jones and Stokes, 2002), chap. 3, 1–2; Erich Obermayr, *Foot Path to Four-Lane: A Historical Guidebook to Transportation on Lake Tahoe's Southeast Shore* (Moundhouse, Nev.: Nevada Department of Transportation, 2005), 21–23; E. B. Scott, *The Saga of Lake Tahoe,* vol. 1, (Crystal Bay, Nev.: Sierra-Tahoe Publishing, 1957), 251.

3. Washoe Tribe, "Protection of De'ek wadapush (Cave Rock)," n.d., www yachaywasi-ngo.org/SC24USAwashoe.pdf (accessed Feb. 12, 2009); FEIS, chap. 3, 9–10. We use the terms *shaman* and *doctor* interchangeably because Washoe sources have consistently done so since the earliest interviews in the 1930s.

4. For an overarching discussion of Indian sacred places, see Vine Deloria Jr., *Spirit and Reason: The Vine Deloria, Jr., Reader* (Golden, Colo.: Fulcrum Publishing, 1999), 323–38; see also Peter Nabokov, *Where the Lightning Strikes: The Lives of American Indian Sacred Places* (New York: Penguin Group, 2006); FEIS, chap. 2, 21.

5. Scott, *The Saga of Lake Tahoe,* vol. 1, 256; FEIS, chap. 3, 1, 13–15. See also Don Handelman, "The Development of a Washoe Shaman," in *Native Californians: A Theoretical Retrospective,* ed. John Lowell Bean and Thomas Blackburn (Menlo Park, Calif.: Ballena Press, 1976); Edgar E. Siskin Papers, Collection 90–68, box 1, Special Collections Department, University of Nevada, Reno [hereafter UNR]. The statement about not driving through the tunnels comes from discussions with numerous tribe members.

6. Obermayr, *Foot Path to Four-Lane,* 12, 22; Scott, *Saga of Lake Tahoe,* vol. 1, 251–56; E. B. Scott, *The Saga of Lake Tahoe,* vol. 2 (Crystal Bay, Nev.: Sierra-Tahoe Publishing, 1973), 64–65.

7. Thomas Frederick Howard, *Sierra Crossing: First Roads to California* (Berke-

ley: University of California Press, 1998), 156; Scott, *Saga of Lake Tahoe,* vol. 2, 62–63; FEIS, chap. 3, 12–13; Scott, *Saga of Lake Tahoe,* vol. 1, 255.

8. Scott, *Saga of Lake Tahoe,* vol. 2, 67.

9. FEIS, chap. 3, 8; Paul McHugh, "The Battle over Cave Rock," *San Francisco Chronicle,* Sept. 25, 2003.

10. Mike Carville, *Rock Climbing Lake Tahoe* (Helena, Mt.: Falcon Books, 1999), 3. The quote is from McHugh, "The Battle over Cave Rock."

11. Carville, *Rock Climbing Lake Tahoe,* 3.

12. Ibid., 112–14, 223–24; FEIS, chap. 3, 30–31. Osman considered Jay Smith one of his four climbing exemplars (Todhunter, *Fall of the Phantom Lord,* 24).

13. Todhunter, *Fall of the Phantom Lord,* 29.

14. Carville, *Rock Climbing Lake Tahoe,* 112; FEIS, chap. 3, 30–33. In 2002 forest managers estimated nonclimbing Cave Rock recreation users at 750–1,000 annual visits (FEIS, 33).

15. FEIS, chap. 1, 2; Washoe Tribal Council Minutes, Apr. 5, 1951, folder 064, Washoe Tribe Minutes, 1945–1955, box 7, Western Nevada Agency, Carson, Tribal Council Minutes/Resolutions 1940–1974, Record Group [hereafter RG] 75, National Archives and Records Administration [hereafter NARA], Pacific Region, San Bruno, Calif.; *Record Courier,* Apr. 20, May 11, 1951; Brian Wallace, Gardnerville, Nev., to Steve Chilton, Aug. 24, 1992, Washoe Tribe of Nevada and California files, Gardnerville; Linda Eissmann, Carson City, Nev., to Brian Wallace, May 28, 1993, Washoe Tribe of Nevada and California files, Gardnerville, Nev.

16. "Cave Rock's Religious Importance," *Tahoe Daily Tribune,* Apr. 18, 1993; Carville, *Rock Climbing Lake Tahoe,* 15.

17. "Cave Rock's Religious Importance," *Tahoe Daily Tribune,* Apr. 18, 1993; Brian Wallace, videotaped interview with Michael Makley, Carson City, Nev., June 14, 1998, video in possession of authors.

18. Sam Davidson, *Access Notes,* vol. 20 (winter 1997), www.accessfund.org (accessed Feb. 22, 1998).

19. "A Brief History of the Access Fund," http://www.accessfund.org/about/history.php (accessed Feb. 24, 2009); www.outdoorlink.com/accessfund/whoweare/board.html (accessed June 15, 1997); National Park Service, *Devils Tower N.M.—Final Climbing Management Plan,* www.nps.gov/archive/deto/deto_climbing/detotoc.html (accessed October 4, 2008).

20. Paul Minault, San Francisco, Calif., to Steve Chilton, July 12, 1993, copy in possession of authors.

21. Juan Palma, "Cave Rock Management Direction, Lake Tahoe Basin Management Unit [hereafter LTBMU], Douglas County, Nev.," *Federal Register* 64, no. 15, Jan. 25, 1999/Notices, 3678–80, 3678; Brian Wallace, Gardnerville, Nev., to Steve Chilton, Aug. 24, 1992, Washoe Tribe of Nevada and California files, Gardner ville, Nev.

22. FEIS, chap. 3, 32; Outdoor Industry Association, *Industry News,* Mar. 30, 2005, www.outdoorindustry.org/media.outdoor.php?news-id=1132&sort-year=2005 (accessed Jan. 21, 2009); Palma, "Cave Rock Management Direction," 3678.

ONE: THE CENTER

1. Earl James, Washoe Tribal Chairman, to Nicholas Allen, Attorney at Law, May 22, 1961, folder 90–37/I/14, Correspondence Jan–July, 1961, box 1, George F. Wright Washoe Claims Case Records, Collection 90–37/I, Special Collections Department, UNR. On the importance of Tahoe, also see James F. Downs, *The Two Worlds of the Washo, an Indian Tribe of California and Nevada* (New York: Holt, Rinehart and Winston, 1966), 16–17.

2. Darrel Bender, videotaped interview with Michael Makley, Carson City, Nev., June 6, 1998, in possession of authors.

3. James F. Downs, "Washo Religion," *University of California Publications: Anthropological Records* 16, no. 9 (1960): 371.

4. Archaeologists identified Cave Rock in the 1950s as likely a component of the Martis Complex, the earliest known local Native culture. But that study and another in 1997 revealed the absence of midden, flake tools, grinding slabs, flakes, or hand stones that would be typical of Martis habitation centers. The scarcity of artifacts, the exotic nature of those found in terms of function and material type, and the absence of debris that characterizes living sites indicated that the items found there were brought to the cave, not made in it. This finding corroborates Washoe accounts, leading to the conclusion that the cave was used for a purpose other than habitation. "Notes and News," *American Antiquity* 23, no. 3 (1958): 330–44, 331–32; Scott, *The Saga of Lake Tahoe,* vol. 1, 256; FEIS, chap. 3, 1, 13–15. Cave Rock is the only Washoe spiritual site that has been studied archaeologically and ethnographically. It was the first excavated site in Douglas County to receive a Smithsonian number (DO-1/University of California at Berkeley; DO-8/Nevada State Museum).

5. Bender, interview with Michael Makley, June 6, 1998.

6. Ibid.

7. Jacob T. Lockhart, Indian Agent, Nevada, to W. P. Dole, Commissioner of Indian Affairs, March 12, 1862, *Letters Received, Nevada Superintendency 1861–1880,* NARA microfilm publications 234, roll 538.

8. Hubbard G. Parker, Superintendent of Indian Affairs, Nevada, to Dennis Cooley, Commissioner of Indian Affairs, September 10, 1866, *Annual Report of the Commissioner of Indian Affairs* (Washington, D.C.: Government Printing Office, 1866), 117.

9. Ibid.

10. The quote comes from Richard Henry Pratt, the American official who created the first Indian boarding school in Carlisle, Pennsylvania, in the late

1880s. For a broad discussion of Indian education, see Margaret Connell Szasz, *Education and the American Indian: The Road to Self-Determination since 1928,* 3rd ed. (Albuquerque: University of New Mexico Press, 1999).

11. For more information on the Washoe experience with the Dawes Act, see Matthew S. Makley, "These Will Be Strong: A History of the Washoe People," Ph.D. diss., Arizona State University, 2007, 95–121.

12. For a discussion on the land purchase, see ibid., 121–59; see also JoAnne Nevers, *Wa She Shu: A Tribal History* (Reno: Inter-tribal Council of Nevada, Reno, 1976), 79; and Susan Wise Ford, "Lorenzo D. Creel and the Purchase of Land," master's thesis, University of Nevada, Reno, 1989, 114.

13. Belma Jones, taped interview with JoAnne Peden, tape G, Woodfords, Calif., Aug. 8, 1992, tape in possession of Barbara Jones, transcript in possession of authors.

14. Dr. S. L. Lee's inventory is in Dr. S. L. Lee Personal Basket Collection, box 5, Warren L. d'Azevedo Washo Indians Research Papers, Collection 99–39, Special Collections Department, UNR; Sam P. Davis, *The History of Nevada* (Reno: Elms Publishing, 1913), 1:131–32; Nevers, *Wa She Shu,* 68–69.

15. R. T. King, "An Interview with Fred Dressler," April 10, 1984, in *Contribution to a Survey of Life in Carson Valley, 1850s–1950s* (Reno: Oral History Program, UNR Library, 1984), 195–97; also King's interview with Bernice Auchoberry, April 3, 1984, 8.

16. Nevers, *Wa She Shu,* 92.

TWO: THE TUNNELS

1. William F. Ogburn, "Inventions and Discoveries," *American Journal of Sociology* 34, no. 1 (1928): 25–39, 25.

2. Frederic L. Paxson, "The Highway Movement, 1916–1935," *American Historical Review* 51, no. 2 (1946): 236–53, 238–39.

3. Obermayr, *Foot Path to Four-Lane,* 10–11. Henry B. Joy, director of the Packard Motor Car Company and president of the Lincoln Highway Association, commented, "What we really had in mind was not to build a road but to procure the building of many roads, by educating people" (10). "Brief History of the Direct Federal Highway Construction Program," Federal Highway Administration, http://www.fhwa.cot.gov/infrastructure/blazer01.htm, 1 (accessed Nov. 14, 2008). A 1915 map of Nevada's principal highways marked not only county seats and towns but also unnamed waterholes along the roads; see H. M. Payne, *Map of Nevada,* 1915, Nevada State Library, Carson City.

4. "Geographical Record," *Geographical Review* 18, no. 2 (1928): 321.

5. *Record Courier,* Jan. 16, 1931; FEIS, chap. 3, 13; State of Nevada, *Ninth Biennial Report of the Department of Highways: For the Period July 1, 1932 to June 30, 1934, Inclusive* (Carson City, Nev.: State Printing Office, 1932), 21.

6. *Record Courier,* May 8, July 24, 1931; FEIS, chap. 3, 13.

7. Darrel Bender, a Washoe elder interviewed in 1998, commented: "Non-Washoe say the Washoes never said anything [about the tunnel blasted in the rock]. They never talked to the Washoe. This is the first time anybody has ever included the Washoe regarding Cave Rock. When they dug the tunnels through there, Washoes were excluded. In those days they didn't talk to Indians." Interview in Mike Makley, video: *Cave Rock: The Issue,* Eastern Sierra Productions, 1998.

8. *Record Courier,* Apr. 17, 1931.

9. *Record Courier,* Apr. 24, 1931.

10. *Record Courier,* June 26, July 24, Aug. 28, Sept. 25, Oct. 2, 1931; "The Zion Tunnel," www.nps.gov/zion/planyourvisit/the-zion-mount-carmel-tunnel.htm (accessed Nov. 5, 2008); William M. Nagel, in Scott, *The Saga of Lake Tahoe,* vol. 2, 67; Warren L. d'Azevedo, "A Note on Cave Rock," Sept. 7, 1992, unpublished manuscript, Hung-a-lel-ti Indian Education Center, Woodfords, Calif.

11. Ignoring Indian concerns regarding traditional sites was typical of government agencies throughout most of the twentieth century. Prior to the 1990s, development at sacred or historically significant properties was allowed and sometimes actively encouraged. See Yablon, "Property Rights and Sacred Sites," *Yale Law Journal* 113, no. 7 (2004): 1623–62, 1627–29.

12. *Record Courier,* June 21, Aug. 9, Sept. 27, 1956; "Brief History of the Direct Federal Highway Construction Program," 3.

13. *Record Courier,* Oct. 18, Dec. 13, 1956, Jan. 3, 1957.

14. *Record Courier,* June 21, 1956, Jan. 3, 31, May 23, July 25, Aug. 8, 1957; State of Nevada, *Eighth Biennial Report of the Department of Highways: For the Period December 1, 1930 to June 30, 1932, Inclusive* (Carson City, Nev.: State Printing Office, 1932), 19.

THREE: REAL POWERS

1. Lee's account is in Dr. S. L. Lee Personal Basket Collection, box 5, p. 13, in d'Azevedo, Washo Indians Research Papers, UNR Library Special Collections.

2. Downs, "Washo Religion," 373.

3. This description of power comes from anthropologists who worked during the 1950s and 1960s with Washoe sources. Stanley A. Freed and Ruth S. Freed, "A Configuration of Aboriginal Washoe Culture," in *The Washoe Indians of California and Nevada,* ed. Warren L. d'Azevedo (Salt Lake City: University of Utah Press—Anthropology Publications, 1963), 41–43; Downs, "Washo Religion," 370; Edgar Siskin, *Washo Shamans and Peyotists: Religious Conflict in an American Indian Tribe* (Salt Lake City: University of Utah Press, 1983), 21; Don Handleman, "Aspects of the Moral Compact of a Washo Shaman," *Anthropological Quarterly* 45, no. 2 (1972): 84–98, 88; Downs, *The Two Worlds of the Washo,* 55–59.

4. Agreement is lacking on gender practice. Darrel Bender claimed that only

men could doctor. Anthropologist Edgar Siskin claimed that both men and women could be shamans, "theoretically in equal number." Siskin tallied recognized practicing Washoe doctors in the early twentieth century based on information from two practicing shamans, Mike Dick and Henry Rupert. Dick knew of ten "full-fledged" shamans, three of whom were women (Becky Jack, Ruth Calley, and Emma Wilson); see Siskin, *Washo Shamans and Peyotists,* 22. Robert Lowie's sources took both sides of the question; see Robert Lowie, "Ethnographic Notes on the Washoe," *University of California Publications in American Archaeology and Ethnology* 36, no. 5 (1939): 319. The federal government's attempt to replace Native gender roles with the patriarchy practiced by Americans muddies the issue.

5. Downs, "Washo Religion," 369; Siskin, *Washo Shamans and Peyotists,* 22, 23, 27; Darrel Bender, videotaped interview with Michael Makley, Carson City, Nev., June 14, 1998, video in possession of authors.

6. Freed and Freed, "A Configuration of Aboriginal Washo Culture," 43; Siskin, *Washo Shamans and Peyotists,* 3–33.

7. Greg Sarris, *Mabel Mckay: Weaving the Dream* (Berkeley: University of California Press, 1994), 30–31.

8. Nabokov, *Where the Lightning Strikes,* 232–35.

9. Downs, "Washo Religion," 370.

10. Siskin, *Washo Shamans and Peyotists,* 27–34.

11. Ibid.

12. Rupert on fasting is in Siskin, *Washo Shamans and Peyotists,* 34; Hank Pete is in Freed and Freed, "A Configuration of Aboriginal Washo Culture," 44.

13. Siskin, *Washo Shamans and Peyotists,* 33, 34.

14. Ibid., 32–33.

15. Warren d'Azevedo, "Washoe," in *The Handbook of North American Indians,* vol. 11, ed. William C. Sturtevant, 489 (Washington, D.C.: Smithsonian Institution, 1986).

16. Siskin, *Washo Shamans and Peyotists,* 44. Anthropologist James Downs presented an account from an unnamed Washoe source that is likely an alternate version of this same story. In Downs' informant's account, the evil doctor, not specifically named, came from northern Washoe country. The informant claimed her aunt had fed the evil doctor, and therefore survived (Downs, "Washo Religion," 372).

17. For a brief version of this story, see Downs, "Washo Religion," 367.

18. Nabokov, *Where the Lightning Strikes,* 227.

19. Chris Peters, "Report of the Native American Sacred Lands Forum," summary of panelists' remarks, Boulder, Colo., Oct. 9–10, 2001, 3, http://www.sacredland.org/pDFs/SL_Forum.final.pdf (accessed Oct. 11, 2008); FEIS, chap. 3, 9–10.

20. Vine Deloria Jr., "Out of Chaos," in *I Become Part of It,* ed. D. M. Dooling and Paul Jordon Smith, 261 (New York: Parabola Books, 1989).

21. Brian Wallace, videotaped interview with Michael Makley, Carson City, Nev., June 14, 1998, video in possession of authors; Lisa Grayshield, videotaped interview with Michael Makley, Carson City, Nev., Sept. 17, 2003, video in possession of authors.

FOUR: THE INNOVATOR

1. FEIS, chap. 2, 9.

2. Handelman, "Aspects of the Moral Compact of a Washo Shaman," 96; Downs, "Washo Religion," 369.

3. Downs, *The Two Worlds of the Washo,* 32–33. Downs noted: "The Washoe considered the bear a very special, if not sacred, animal possessed of enormous supernatural power" (33). It is of no small significance that one of Rupert's earliest dreams involved a bear. Also see Handelman, "The Development of a Washoe Shaman," 381. In the late 1930s a graduate student in anthropology from Yale University, Edgar E. Siskin, spent three summers working with the Washoes. He put together copious amounts of information, much of which is housed in the Special Collections Department at the University of Nevada, Reno. His handwritten field notes include information from "Charlie," listed as "C.R." in Siskin's list of informants and probably Charlie Rube. For Rube's full description of the sacred nature of bears in Washoe culture, see Edgar E. Siskin Field Notes, June 25, 1937, Edgar E. Siskin Papers, Collection 90–68, box 1, Special Collections Department, UNR.

4. Freed and Freed, "A Configuration of Aboriginal Washoe Culture," 53; Downs, "Washo Religion," 379. Warren d'Azevedo pointed out that Edgar Siskin and James Downs believed "leadership of antelope drives was essentially secular and could be held by any proficient hunter." Downs described an antelope shamanistic complex throughout the Great Basin "surrounded by an aura of sacredness and ritual." He claimed a "man with special power, an antelope shaman," could attract antelope, although he said there was no "special antelope shaman" among the Washoes; see Downs, *The Two Worlds of the Washo,* 32. D'Azevedo, drawing on his own fieldwork and the work of Robert Lowie and Grace Dangberg, suggested Downs and Siskin were not correct. He recalled a "few older Washoes in the 1950s [who] knew traditional accounts of special individuals who led antelope drives and were designated . . . antelope doctor or shaman." See d'Azevedo, "Washoe," in *The Handbook of North American Indians,* 488. Don Handelman in "The Development of a Washoe Shaman" did not address whether or not the office of antelope shaman existed, he simply described Charlie Rube as "an antelope shaman, a man who in aboriginal times was entrusted with the task of 'singing' antelope to sleep during the annual Washoe antelope drives" (380).

Handelman likely obtained his information from Henry Rupert. For the account of Hudson, see J. W. Hudson, Correspondence and Field Notes ca. 1902, folder 99–39, box 5, 247, d'Azevedo, Washo Indians Research Papers.

5. Lowie, "Ethnographic Notes on the Washoe," 324–25; d'Azevedo, "Washoe," in Smithsonian Collection, 478.

6. Handelman, "The Development of a Washoe Shaman," 381.

7. Freed and Freed, "A Configuration of Aboriginal Washoe Culture," 44. The Freeds claimed Hank Pete had told them the story of Welewkushkush. Hank Pete, the son of Captain Pete, the Washoes' leader in the late nineteenth and early twentieth centuries, was elected to the first Washoe Tribal Council in 1936 and played a pivotal role in initiating the land claims case in the 1940s. For a treatment of the Washoe land claims case, see Matthew S. Makley, "These Will Be Strong: A History of the Washoe People."

8. Handelman, "The Development of a Washoe Shaman," 382.

9. Siskin, *Washo Shamans and Peyotists,* 175.

10. W. D. C. Gibson, Superintendent, Commissioner of Indian Affairs, September 7, 1891, in *Annual Report of the Commissioner of Indian Affairs* (Washington, D.C.: Government Printing Office, 1892).

11. John H. Oberly, Commissioner of Indian Affairs, *Fifty-seventh Annual Report of the Commissioner of Indian Affairs to the Secretary of the Interior, 1888* (Washington, D.C.: Government Printing Office, 1888), xix.

12. Roberta Snyder, videotaped interview with Michael Makley, Carson City, Nev., Sept. 17, 1998, video in possession of authors.

13. "Rules and Regulations of the Court of Indian Offenses at the Nevada Agency." Fred B. Spriggs, U.S. Indian agent for the Nevada Agency, approved the creation of a court of Indian offenses and set nineteen rules to be governed by the court; see Walker River Agency Correspondence, 1906–32, box 252, RG75, NARA Regional Branch, San Bruno, Calif.

14. Handelman, "The Development of a Washoe Shaman," 385; see also Freed and Freed, "A Configuration of Aboriginal Culture," 43. Rupert worked with Handelman and the Freeds, and he likely explained his power dream to them. Their versions vary, but whether because Rupert altered his description or the Freeds and Handelman interpreted it differently is unknown. The Freeds described the voice in the dream as a "talking deer," but Handelman claimed the voice came from a snake who was "warning against the indiscriminate taking of life; previously Henry had killed wildlife, insects, and snakes without much concern."

15. "Rules and Regulations of the Court of Indian Offenses at the Nevada Agency."

16. Siskin, *Washo Shamans and Peyotists,* 176; Handelman, *The Development of a Washo Shaman,* 387, 398–99; Downs, *The Two Worlds of the Washo,* 56; see also

Handelman, "Trans-cultural Shamanic Healing: A Washoe Example," *Ethnos* 32 (1967): 162. Handelman, in "Trans-cultural Shamanic Healing" (162), identified Rupert's source on hypnotism as *The Art of Attention and the Science of Suggestion,* which he claimed Rupert studied for two years beginning in 1907.

17. Washoe Census, March 13, 1917, "Carson" folder, box 2, Nevada Investigative Records of Col. L. A. Dorrington, Special Agent, 1913–1923, RG 75, NARA, San Bruno, Calif.

18. Siskin, *Washo Shamans and Peyotists,* 202.

19. Ibid., 30–31, 34–35.

20. Handelman described Rupert's encounter with Lowie in "The Development of a Washoe Shaman," 388. See the original citation in Lowie, "Ethnographic Notes on the Washoe," 321.

21. Handleman, "The Development of a Washoe Shaman," 390.

22. Ibid.

23. Ibid., 392.

24. John Pohland, Clerk, Special Indian Agent, to Henry Rupert, February 10, 1917, folder 459, Gardnerville, box 10, Nevada Reno Indian Agency Records of Agency and Non-agency Indians, Tribal Groups from Bishop Sub-agency, RG 75, NARA, San Bruno, Calif.

25. Henry Rupert to Indian Agent, February 8, 1917, folder 459, Gardnerville, box 10, Nevada Reno Indian Agency Records of Agency and Non-agency Indians, Tribal Groups from Bishop Sub-agency, RG 75, NARA, San Bruno, Calif.

26. Washoe Census, March 13, 1917, "Carson" folder, box 2, Nevada Investigative Records of Col. L. A. Dorrington, Special Agent, 1913–23, NARA, San Bruno, Calif.

27. Handelman, "The Development of a Washoe Shaman," 395.

28. Ibid., 391, 396–97; Downs, "Washo Religion," 369; see also Handelman, "Trans-cultural Shamanic Healing," 151–53. Sixty-nine percent of the patients came from Nevada; the remaining 31 percent lived in California. Washoes comprised 56 percent; Northern Paiutes made up about 20 percent; the remaining 24 percent were almost evenly spread among Shoshones, Euro-Americans, and Others (defined as Mexican and Hawaiian).

29. Handelman, "The Development of a Washoe Shaman," 398.

30. Ibid., 398–403.

31. Downs, "Washo Religion," 369.

32. FEIS, chap. 2, 9.

FIVE: SLAYER

1. Lawrence C. Hamilton, "Modern American Rock: Some Aspects of Social Change," *Pacific Sociological Review* 22, no. 3 (1979): 285–308, 285–86, 291

2. Therese C. Grijalva, Robert P. Berrens, Alok K. Bohara, Paul M. Jakus, and

W. Douglass Shaw, "Valuing the Loss of Rock Climbing Access in Wilderness Areas: A National-Level, Random-Utility Model," *Land Economics* 78, no. 1 (2002): 103–20, 104–5.

3. Hamilton, "Modern American Rock," 295–96.

4. Ibid., 288–89; Carville, *Rock Climbing Lake Tahoe,* 3; Richard Rossiter, *Rock Climbing the Flatirons* (Guilford, Conn.: Globe Pequot, 1999), 4.

5. FEIS, chap. 3, 42–43.

6. Todhunter, *Fall of the Phantom Lord,* 70; Carville, *Rock Climbing Lake Tahoe,* 3; *Los Angeles Times,* Oct. 18, 1993; Hamilton, "Modern American Rock," 290.

7. "Hot Flashes," *Climbing,* no. 132 (June–July 1992): 39.

8. Rebecca Noyes, videotaped interview with Michael Makley, South Lake Tahoe, May 27, 1998, video in possession of authors.

9. Todhunter, *Fall of the Phantom Lord,* 3, 11, 13, 24–26, 74. Osman's popularity with sponsors was easy to understand. Todhunter described one poster of him as follows: "He holds himself perpendicular to a near-vertical rock face, a gymnastic pose called a horizontal press. His hands are wide, one above the other. His arms are straight, locked at the elbow. His feet are together, his toes pointed like a diver's. His body, parallel to the earth, is as straight as a pike. He is unroped, far from the ground." The poster reads, "Reality is in fact virtual" (*Fall of the Phantom Lord,* 117).

10. Ibid., 201.

11. Perrie Arens, interview with Michael Makley, Woodfords, Calif., Apr. 7, 2009; Todhunter, *Fall of the Phantom Lord,* 172.

12. "Tributo a Dan Osman," subtitled in Italian, http://www.youtube.com/watch?v=_jKA_csRaew&feature=related (accessed Mar. 3, 2009); Todhunter, *Fall of the Phantom Lord,* 108.

13. Placing a difficult route can take many months because the builder has to puzzle over alternative moves and unique techniques; see Todhunter, *Fall of the Phantom Lord,* 18, 62–63.

14. Carville, *Rock Climbing Lake Tahoe,* 115, 224; Todhunter, *Fall of the Phantom Lord,* 18, 29.

15. Todhunter, *Fall of the Phantom Lord,* 18, 29–32; "Hot Flashes," 39.

16. Todhunter, *Fall of the Phantom Lord,* 27; "Hot Flashes," 39; John Maher, quoted in "The Battle over Cave Rock," *San Francisco Chronicle,* Sept. 25, 2003.

17. Craig Vetter, "Terminal Velocity," *Outside* (April 1999), http://outside.away.com/magazine/0499/index.html (accessed Sept. 23, 2008).1–2, 5; Todhunter, *Fall of the Phantom Lord,* 31–32, 53. Osman's technical, high-risks falls from the promontory at the Lower Cave area while secured by his rope and harness led to reports of bungee jumping at Cave Rock (FEIS, chap. 3, 34)

18. "Tributo a Dan Osman"; Todhunter, *Fall of the Phantom Lord,* 13.

19. Vetter, "Terminal Velocity," 1-2, 5; Todhunter, *Fall of the Phantom Lord,* 32-33.

20. A 1998 title search back to the original patent documented the 1996 deter-

mination. See *Cave Rock Management Direction Draft Environmental Impact Statement* [hereafter DEIS] (Douglas County, Nev.: Lake Tahoe Basin Management Unit, 1999), chap. 1, 2.

21. Federal Historic Preservation Case Law, 1966–96, http://www.achp.gov/book/sectionVI.html (accessed Nov. 26, 2008); regarding Executive Order 13007, see Indian Sacred Sites, May 24, 1996, http://www.achp.gov/EO13007.html (accessed Oct. 9, 2008); "Decision Documentation, to Support the Area Closure," Cave Rock Closure for Resource Protection, USDA/OES, ID 2027202166, Dec. 9, 1997, 7–8; Dave Allasia, interview with Michael J. Makley, Woodfords, Calif., Feb. 3, 2009; FEIS, chap. 1, 3–4.

22. Todhunter, *Fall of the Phantom Lord,* 192–93.

23. *Tahoe Daily Tribune,* May 28, 1997; *Access Notes,* vol. 18 (summer 1997), www.accessfund.org (accessed Feb. 22, 1998).

24. Vetter, "Terminal Velocity," 1, 6; "Tributo a Dan Osman."

SIX: HUNTER-GATHERERS AND COURTS

1. Much of the following discussion of the government's management of sacred sites is based on Yablon, "Property Rights and Sacred Sites."

2. *Johnson v. M'Intosh,* 21 U.S. 543, 5 L.E.d. 681, 8 Wheat. 543 (1823); see also Yablon, "Property Rights and Sacred Sites," 1634–36; Richard Herz, "Legal Protection for Indigenous Cultures: Sacred Sites and Communal Rights," *Virginia Law Review* 79, no. 3 (1993): 691–716, 705–6. Legal scholar Lloyd Burton pointed out that the term *Indian* is still in use five hundred years after it became known that the indigenous people of North and South America had nothing to do with India. Lloyd suggested that using the term implied that the original inhabitants did not really belong here: "It was important for the immigrants to see the indigenes not as native but as foreign," so the land could be expropriated. See Lloyd Burton, *Worship and Wilderness: Culture, Religion, and Law in the Management of Public Lands and Resources* (Madison: University of Wisconsin Press, 2002), 23, 167. Historian Patricia Nelson Limerick asserted that white settlers thought the Indians were wasting resources in not putting the land to its proper use, and contended *they* "were philanthropic and farsighted in wanting to liberate the land" (Patricia Nelson Limerick, *The Legacy of Conquest: The Unbroken Past of the American West* [New York: W. W. Norton, 1987], 90).

3. G. Jon Roush, President, Wilderness Society, to *New York Times,* July 15, 1994; J. Brennan, "Dissenting Opinion," *Lyng v. Northwest Indian Cemetery Protective Association,* 485 U.S. 439 (1988).

4. Yablon, "Property Rights and Sacred Sites," 1627; David Kent Sproul, *A Bridge between Cultures: An Administrative History of Rainbow Bridge National Monument* (Denver: National Park Service, 2001), 220–28.

5. Yablon, "Property Rights and Sacred Sites," 1624–25; Burton, *Worship and Wilderness,* 45.

6. Yablon, "Property Rights and Sacred Sites," 1625–27; Robert S. Michaelsen, "American Indian Religious Freedom Litigation: Promise and Perils," *Journal of Law and Religion* 3, no. 1 (1985): 47–76, 47; Burton, *Worship and Wilderness,* 158–61; Student Environmental Action Coalition, "Mount Graham," www.seac.org/seac-sw/mtg.htm (accessed Nov. 24, 2008).

7. Herz, "Legal Protection for Indigenous Cultures," 705; Yablon, "Property Rights and Sacred Sites," 1628–29; Burton, *Worship and Wilderness,* 15.

8. Michaelsen, "American Indian Religious Freedom Litigation," 57; "American Indian Religious Freedom and Native American Graves and Repatriation and Protection Act," DOE Environmental Policy and Guidance, http://www.hss.energy.gov/nuclearsafety/nsea/oepa/laws/airfa082505.html (accessed Dec. 22, 2008).

9. Herz, "Legal Protection for Indigenous Cultures," 706; "*Lyng v. Northwest Indian Cemetery Protective Association,*" Syllabus, Supreme Court of the United States, Supreme Court Collection, Cornell University Law School, http://www.law.cornell.edu/supct/html/histories/USSC_CR_0485_0439_ZS.hml (accessed Nov. 12, 2008).

10. For an excellent treatment of the Indian movement of the 1960s and 1970s, see Paul Chaat Smith and Roger Allen Warrior, *Like a Hurricane: The Indian Movement from Alcatraz to Wounded Knee* (New York: New Press, 1996).

11. Yablon, "Property Rights and Sacred Sites," 1638–39, 1646; Secretary of Agriculture Dan Glickman, preface to *Guide to USDA Programs for American Indians and Alaska Natives,* http://www.usda.gov/news/pubs/indians/preface.htm (accessed Oct. 14, 2008). Congress actually began to atone for earlier U.S. policies in 1978 by passing the American Indian Religious Freedom Act (AIRFA). When fears arose that the bill might allow preferential treatment to tribes, the bill's sponsor, Representative Morris Udall, argued that the law merely presented a "sense of Congress" and "has no teeth in it." Subsequent court decisions proved him correct (see Burton, *Worship and Wilderness,* 108–9). Government agencies nevertheless cite this and other acts and executive actions when deciding cases, as in the original closure of Cave Rock in 1997, when the forest supervisor cited AIRFA, the National Historic Preservation Act, and Clinton's executive order on Indian sacred sites ("Cave Rock Closure for Resource Protection," USDA/OES, Dec. 9, 1997, 7–9).

12. Burton, *Worship and Wilderness,* 147–50; Yablon, "Property Rights and Sacred Sites," 1636–38. Yablon argued that agencies are better suited to enforce the rules because they have to make site-specific regulations, and that cases like Bear Lodge "would not have been appropriate for most or even many other sacred sites" (1658).

13. Burton, *Worship and Wilderness,* 4, 8–9, 123–24.

14. Ibid., 135–38.

15. Yablon, "Property Rights and Sacred Sites," 1623–24, 1648; Burton, *Worship and Wilderness,* 137–41, 167.

16. Jefferson 21st Century Institute, "Archive of Threats to Separation of Religion and Government," http://www.j21c.org/threats1.htm (accessed Nov. 12, 2008); William Perry Pendley, "Feds Establish Religion on 'Sacred' Indian Site," Jul. 28, 2000, http://findarticles.com/p/articles/mi_qa3827/is_/ai_n8904612.

17. Associated Press, "10th Circuit: Forest Service Can Bar Logging near Medicine Wheel," Sept. 21, 2004; Yablon, "Property Rights and Sacred Sites," 1651–53; Burton, *Worship and Wilderness,* 161–64.

18. Burton, *Worship and Wilderness,* 165–69; Yablon, "Property Rights and Sacred Sites," 1652–53.

19. Besides identifying goodwill as a concern, scholar Marcia Yablon named four benefits of government agencies being charged with the decision-making responsibility rather than the judicial and legislative branches: (1) the protection offered by agencies is site-specific, so not overly inclusive; (2) because agencies are closer to disputed areas they can better understand the issues and forge compromise; (3) agencies are free from the property rules that courts are obliged to follow; and (4) agencies are not forced into zero-sum decisions, but rather can accommodate land use that does not foreclose all other uses (Yablon, "Property Rights and Sacred Sites," 1658–60).

SEVEN: COMMON OR UNCOMMON GROUND

1. Davidson, *Access Notes,* vol. 19 (fall 1997).

2. *Access Notes,* vol. 20 (winter 1997). One writer attacked Davidson from the other side, saying he supported access "pure-and-simple" and was "very disturbed that the analyst had presented the attitude of 'victimized' Native Americans."

3. Ibid.

4. The Lake Tahoe Basin Management Unit was formed in 1973 by combining parts of three national forests that reached into the Tahoe basin in order to facilitate planning and protection for the lake and provide a unified approach to public land management.

5. Juan Palma, video recording, Cave Rock Collaboration Effort Meeting 3, Carson City, Mar. 17, 1998, video in possession of authors; "Juan Palma Named Director of BLM's Eastern States Office," Bureau of Land Management press release, November 29, 2007, http://www.blm.gov/wo/st/en/info/newroom/2007/0711/NR_07_11_29.print.html (accessed Oct. 5, 2008).

6. "Differences Are Monumental in Cave Rock Dispute," *Chicago Sun-Times,* May 18, 1997.

7. *Access Notes,* vol. 18 (summer 1997).

8. Juan Palma, video recording, Cave Rock Collaboration Effort Meeting 5, South Lake Tahoe, Calif., May 27, 1998, video in possession of authors; "Climb-

ing Ban Fails," *High Country News,* June 23, 1997; *Tahoe Daily Tribune,* May 26, 28, 1997.

9. *Tahoe Daily Tribune,* May 28, 1997.

10. FEIS, chap. 1, 8–9.

11. *Access Notes,* vol. 18 (summer 1997); *Tahoe Daily Tribune,* July 11, 2003.

12. *Tahoe Daily Tribune,* May 28, 1997.

13. Ibid.

14. Ibid.; Emily Miller, *High Country News,* June 23, 1997.

15. Washoe Tribe, "Protection of De'ek wadapush (Cave Rock)"; DEIS, chap. 2, 2; Penny Rucks, telephone interview with Michael Makley, Jan. 31, 2009.

16. Penny Rucks, Heritage Resource Program manager, to Brian Wallace, Sept. 11, 1996; Penny Rucks, telephone interview with Michael Makley, Jan. 31, 2009; Palma, "Cave Rock Management Direction"; DEIS, chap. 1, 1.

17. For examples of Wallace's statements, see Brian Wallace, Gardnerville, Nev., to Steve Chilton, Aug. 24, 1992, Washoe Tribe of Nevada and California files, Gardnerville, Nev.; "Cave Rock's Religious Importance," *Tahoe Daily Tribune,* Apr. 18, 1993; *Tahoe Daily Tribune,* May 28, 1997; and Jan Cutts, "Meeting Process and Content," Meeting 2, Mar. 10, 1998, and Meeting 4, Apr. 9, 1998, FEIS, appendix A, 3–5; DEIS, chap. 3, 73.

18. Cutts, "Meeting Process and Content," Meeting 1, Jan. 22, 1998, FEIS, appendix A, 2.

19. Ibid.; FEIS, chap. 3, 16.

20. Cutts, "Meeting Process and Content," Meeting 2, Mar. 10, 1998, FEIS, appendix A, 2–3; Video recording, Cave Rock Collaboration Effort Meeting 2, Carson City, Nev., Mar. 10, 1998.

21. Cutts, "Meeting Process and Content," Meeting 2, Mar. 10, 1998, FEIS, appendix A, 2–3.

22. "Proposal from Climbers at Discussion Session 3," handout given to participants at Cave Rock Collaboration Effort Meeting 3, Mar. 17, 1998, copy in possession of authors.

23. Brian Wallace, videotaped interview with Michael Makley, Carson City, June 14, 1998.

24. Video recording, Cave Rock Collaboration Effort Meeting 3, Carson City, Nev., Mar. 17, 1998.

25. Ibid.; Cutts, "Meeting Process and Content," Meeting 2, Mar. 17, 1998, FEIS, appendix A, 3–4.

26. Cutts, "Meeting Process and Content," Meeting 4, Apr. 9, 1998, FEIS, appendix A, 4–5; Washoe Tribe, "Protection of De'ek wadapush (Cave Rock)."

27. Makley, video: *Cave Rock: The Issue.*

28. Rebecca Noyes, videotaped interview with Michael Makley, South Lake Tahoe, Calif., May 27, 1998, video in possession of authors; Terry Lilienfield,

videotaped interview with Michael Makley, South Lake Tahoe, Calif., May 27, 1998, video in possession of authors.

29. Juan Palma, Cave Rock Collaboration Effort Meeting 5, video recording, South Lake Tahoe, May 27, 1998, video in possession of authors.

EIGHT: ADVERSE EFFECTS

1. Lisa O'Daly, Cave Rock Collaboration Effort Meeting 5, video recording, South Lake Tahoe, May 27, 1998, video in possession of authors; Lilienfield, interview with Michael Makley, May 27, 1998.

2. DEIS, chap. 1, 4, chap. 3, 38; FEIS, chap. 3, 3–4.

3. Paul Minault, San Francisco, to Juan Palma, Nov. 4, 1998, Washoe Tribe of Nevada and California files, Gardnerville, Nev.

4. Palma, "Cave Rock Management Direction"; Paul Minault to Juan Palma, Nov. 4, 1998.

5. Brian Wallace, interview with Michael Makley, June 14, 1998. A number of participants advocated the idea that climbing is a religious experience. In an editorial about Cave Rock, Access Fund Senior Analyst Sam Davidson wrote: "Many climbers, in their own way, consider our boulders, crags, and mountains holy places" (*Access Notes,* vol. 19 [fall 1997]).

6. DEIS, chap. 3, 70.

7. Eric Perlman to Lake Tahoe Management Unit, Aug. 31, 1999, FEIS, appendix B, n.p.

8. "Juan Palma Named Director of BLM's Eastern States Office," BLM press release, November 29, 2007; Mary Adelzadeh, "Empowerment in an Era of Self-Determination: The Case of the Washoe Tribe and U.S. Forest Service Co-management Agreement," master's thesis, University of Michigan, August 2006, 53–60.

9. Juan Palma, USFS, Lake Tahoe Basin Management Unit, "Cave Rock Management Direction Proposed Action," Jan. 13, 1999.

10. Penny Rucks, Reno, Nev., to Juan Palma, Feb. 23, 1999; Carol Gleichman, "Nevada: Preservation of Cave Rock, Lake Tahoe," May 6, 2003.

11. Penny Rucks, Reno, Nev., to Juan Palma, Feb. 23, 1999.

12. DEIS, Abstract, n.p.

13. Ibid., chap. 2, 5–9.

14. Ibid., chap. 2, 14.

15. Ibid., chap. 3, 38–39. This is also the first indication in the DEIS that members of the public had challenged the finding regarding the site's integrity. The challenge questioned "whether a site that contained two highway tunnels blasted through its center and heavily influenced by the noise of traffic flowing through those two tunnels could retain 'integrity,' as required by the regulations" (chap. 3, 15). The comment is repeated in chap. 3, 38.

16. DEIS, chap. 3, 15, 38–40.

17. Ibid., chap. 2, 14, chap. 3, 15, 38–40.

18. The discussion constitutes the first half of the section titled "Social/Civil Rights Impact Analysis," 3.8(a) "Affected Environment." The DEIS text is numbered incorrectly: 3.8(a) on page 69 is followed by 3.7(b) on page 72, leading to 3.8(a) again on page 76. The next section is correctly labeled 3.9(b) on page 88.

19. DEIS, chap. 3, 69–70.

20. Ibid., chap. 3, 74.

21. Ibid., chap. 3, 39, 52, 69–74. Another section of the chapter quotes two paragraphs from a rock-climbing ethics document and notes that some climbers might follow those guidelines and avoid Cave Rock out of respect for its sacredness to the Washoes (60).

22. DEIS, "References," 96–97.

NINE: REACTIONS

1. FEIS, appendix B, n.p.

2. Ibid.

3. Ibid. Wallace pointed out that the National Historical Preservation Act requires an adequate degree of mitigation, citing the Ninth Circuit Court's discussion in *Muckleshoot Tribe v. U.S. Forest Service* (wherein a land exchange would not adequately protect an important traditional Indian trail) indicating that mitigation that preserves a site's historic features is required where it is possible.

4. Ibid.

5. Ibid.

6. DEIS, chap. 3, 4.

7. FEIS, appendix B, n.p.

8. Terry Lilienfield, South Lake Tahoe, Calif., to Juan Palma, Sept. 22, 1999, FEIS, appendix B, n.p.; *Las Vegas Sun,* July 13, 1999.

9. Carol Gleichman, ACHP Case Digest, "Nevada: Preservation of Cave Rock, Lake Tahoe," May 6, 2003, http://www.achp.gov/casearchive/caseswin03NV.html (accessed Dec. 17, 2008).

10. Ibid.

TEN: RECORD OF DECISION

1. "Maribeth Gustafson to Head White River National Forest," news release, Lake Tahoe Basin management Unit, Feb. 11, 2005; Dave Allasia, interview with Michael Makley, Woodfords, Calif., Feb. 4, 2009; John Maher, telephone interview with Michael Makley, Feb. 27, 2009; Washoe Tribe, "Protection of De'ek wadapush (Cave Rock)"; "Forest Service Extends Its Comment Period for Cave Rock Closure," *Virtual Times* 26 (Dec. 2002), www.accessfund.org/pubs/en

e-news26.html (accessed Feb. 12, 2009); Maribeth Gustafson, telephone interview with Michael J. Makley, Jan. 9, 2009.

2. Executive Order 13175, *Federal Register* 65, no. 218, Nov. 9, 2000, 67249–52.

3. Yablon, "Property Rights and Sacred Sites," 1640–41; 36 C.F.R. 219.9, *Electronic Code of Federal Regulations,* Jan. 27, 2009, "Title 36: Parks, Forests, and Public Property, (3) Engaging Tribal Governments and Alaska Native Corporations" (accessed Jan. 28, 2009).

4. FEIS, chap. 1, 5, 8–9.

5. Associated Press report, Sept. 30, 2002; *Los Angeles Times,* Aug. 20, 2003; Matt Weiser, "Gold May Bury Tribe's Trail to the Past," *High Country News,* Dec. 17, 2001. California senator Barbara Boxer protested that the mine would alter the face of the landscape and "rip the heart out of the Tribe's religious center." The California legislature passed a bill in its 2002 session that would block the project. Hours before the deadline to act at the close of the session, Governor Gray Davis, a Democrat, vetoed the bill. But he directed his staff to pursue other remedies to oppose the mining company and Interior Department, tying up the issue in litigation for years.

6. Gleichman, "Nevada: Land and Resource Management Plan Amendment to Protect Cave Rock."

7. "Forest Service Extends Its Comment Period for Cave Rock Closure," *Virtual Times* 26.

8. Maribeth Gustafson, "Record of Decision for Cave Rock Management Direction," Jul. 8, 2003, 7; FEIS, chap. 2, 7–9.

9. "Cave Rock Decision Announced," news release, Lake Tahoe Basin Management Unit, July 10, 2003. The FEIS includes the discussion of Washoe religion and Cave Rock, and concludes, in an argument later corroborated by the Ninth Circuit Court of Appeals, that discussion of the property in religious terms "does not diminish the site's historical or cultural significance to the Washoe people." Left out of the discussion in the FEIS was the paragraph from the DEIS regarding the Establishment Clause. To compare the two, see FEIS, chap. 3, 50–51, and DEIS, chap. 3, 69–70.

10. Washoe Tribe, "Protection of De'ek wadapush (Cave Rock)"; "Forest Service Extends Its Comment Period for Cave Rock Closure," *Virtual Times* 26; Maribeth Gustafson, "Record of Decision," appendix A, 1.

11. Ibid., 1, 8–9.

12. Ibid., 2, 4, 6, 7; *Tahoe Daily Tribune,* July 11, 2003.

13. Gustafson, "Record of Decision," appendix A, 2, 5. Gustafson was consistent in her assertions. The *Tahoe Daily Tribune* for July 11, 2003, quoted her as saying: "I'm disappointed in the focus of the discussion being the Washoe versus climbers. I've been consistent in my review of this situation, consistent with the

forest plan and its direction. There were a number of attempts to come up with a compromise, none of which protected the resource."

14. Gustafson, "Record of Decision," appendix A, 2, 3, 8.

15. Ibid., 3, 7.

16. Ibid., 4, 9.

ELEVEN: NEW DIRECTIONS

1. Kent P. Connaughton to Terry Lilienfield, "Appeal Decision," Nov. 5, 2003.

2. *Tahoe Daily Tribune,* Sept. 11, Dec. 16, 2003.

3. Ibid.; "Cave Rock Q & A," Access Fund, www.accessfund.org/pdf/CRQA3–28.pdf (accessed Feb. 12, 2009).

4. *Tahoe Daily Tribune,* Dec. 16, 2003.

5. Bill Faulk, "Western Shoshone Elder Jailed," Apr. 20, 1993, http://nativenet.uthscsa.edu/archive/nl/9304/0123.html (accessed Mar. 9, 2009); Scott Robert Ladd, "Stealing Nevada," Sept. 10, 1996, http://ncseonline.org/nae/docs/shoshone.html (accessed Mar. 9, 2009); Associated Press, "Government Proceeds with Indian Cattle Auction," May 31, 2002; *United States and Pyramid Lake Paiute Tribe of Indians v. Alpine Land and Reservoir Company,* 340F.3d 903 (Ninth Circuit 2003).

6. Ryan Slattery, "Men Who Stole Petroglyphs Sentenced to Prison," *Indian Country Today,* Sept. 27, 2004, http://www.coloradoaim.org/blog/2004/09/articles-september-28.html (accessed Feb. 27, 2009).

7. "Cave Rock Management Direction: Hearing in U.S. District Court, Nevada," Feb. 1, 2005, www.fs.fed.us/r3/spf/tribal/documents/caveroc-020205.rtf (accessed Oct. 5, 2008); John Maher, telephone interview with Michael Makley, Feb. 27, 2009. The same-day decision led some to believe that the verdict had been preordained. A board member of one climbers' coalition commented: "Apparently, the Judge has already made up his mind based on [a case] which was very different from the Cave Rock facts"; see Dave Wilson, "Southeast Climbers Coalition Message Board," n.d., http://www.seclimbers.org/modules.php?name=Forums&file=viewtopic&t=6017&view=next (accessed Jan. 21, 2009).

8. *Tahoe Bonanza,* Feb. 2, 2005.

9. Outdoor Industry Association, "Industry News," Mar. 30, 2005, www.outdoorindustry.org/media.outdoor.php?news-id=1132&sort-year=2005 (accessed Jan. 21, 2009).

10. "Tribal Relations: 9th Circuit Court of Appeals Opinion on Cave Rock," Aug. 27, 2007, http://www.fs.fed.us/r5/tribalrelations/caverock.php?more=9cc0a00cr (accessed Oct. 5, 2008).

11. For a discussion of the *Lemon* test, see First Amendment Center, "Religious Liberty in Public Life," n.d., http://www.firstamendmentcenter.org/rel_liberty/free_exercise/index.aspx (accessed Feb. 22, 2009); "Tribal Relations: 9th Circuit Court of Appeals Opinion on Cave Rock," Aug. 27, 2007.

12. *Tahoe Daily Tribune,* Apr. 5, 2004.

13. "Tribal Relations: 9th Circuit Court of Appeals Opinion on Cave Rock," Aug. 27, 2007.

14. Ibid.

15. Robert Stern, edited and updated by Nate Chappelle, "Cave Rock, Nev. (Washo) (2006)," *The Pluralism Project at Harvard University,* July 12, 2006, 6, http://www.pluralism.org/research/profiles/display.php?profile=744332 (accessed Nov. 5, 2008); "Tribal Relations: 9th Circuit Court of Appeals Opinion on Cave Rock," Aug. 27, 2007. For a discussion of *Van Orden,* see http://www.law.cornell.edu/supct/html/03–1500.ZS.html. Even after the final court decision there were those who promoted a convoluted message regarding Cave Rock. William Perry Pendley of the Mountain States Legal Foundation titled his summary of the findings: "Ninth Circuit: Feds May Close Land for Indian Worship!" See Mountain States Legal Foundation, Sept. 1, 2007, http://www.mountainstateslegal.org/summary-judgment.cfm?articleid=116 (accessed Feb. 3, 2009). Pendley claimed that the Judeo-Christian religion had been barred from the "public square" for nearly four decades. He either had not read Judge Wallace's concurrence or somehow overlooked the fact that *Van Orden,* which Wallace had followed, was about the government condoning the placement of a Judeo-Christian monument in a public square. Pendley also ignored Judge McKeown's analysis to declare that in the court's eyes "American Indian religion was uniquely exempt from the Establishment Clause." These assertions led to an astounding conclusion: "Indeed, the Forest Service is not demanding that non-Indians simply 'respect' American Indian religion; it is, in the Court's words, 'employ[ing] the machinery of the state to enforce [Washoe] religious orthodoxy.'" Pendley did not cite a source for the quote regarding "the Court's words."

TWELVE: CONNECTIONS

1. *Tahoe Bonanza,* Feb. 2, 2005; John Maher, telephone interview with Michael Makley, Feb. 27, 2009.

2. See Yablon, "Property Rights and Sacred Sites," 1658–60.

3. Palma's view is presented in the DEIS, chap. 3, 73; Gustafson, "Record of Decision," 5.

4. The latest episode at San Francisco Peaks exemplifies the nearly unbroken history of losses. The Arizona ski area built at the site wants to utilize recycled water containing some human waste to make snow. Hopi and Navajo litigants claim this desecrates the property. The eleven judges sitting en banc on the Ninth Circuit Court of Appeals found in favor of the resort, citing a phrase in the Religious Freedom Restoration Act that says an action must "substantially burden the exercise" of a religion to make it unlawful. The court ruled that the resort's action would have to deny practitioners the use of the site to substantially bur-

den their rights. At this writing, the Native practitioners have appealed the case to the Supreme Court. See Vikram David Amar and Alan Brownstein, "The Navajo Nation Case," Feb. 17, 2009, http://writ.news.findlaw.com/amar/20090217.html (accessed Feb. 26, 2009).

5. Outdoor Industry Association, "Industry News," Mar. 30, 2005.

AFTERWORD

1. DEIS, 75.

2. The information in this chapter comes from John Dayberry, interview with Michael Makley, Sept. 29, 2009. Climbers had used all sorts of jimmied devices to set anchors—such as securing a nut onto a bolt with gobs of silicone.

3. Dayberry built a twenty-foot-by-four-foot sheet-metal flume from used roofing material to carry the debris to a container parked at the edge of the roadway. It took the crew a day of shoveling to remove it all.

BIBLIOGRAPHY

ARCHIVES AND MANUSCRIPT COLLECTIONS

National Archives and Records Administration, Pacific Region, San Bruno, California. Record Group 75, General Records of the Bureau of Indian Affairs.

Administrative Files [first series], 1907–1926. Records of Indian Students, boxes 262–77.

Administrative Records of the Stewart Indian School. Employee Records, 1890–1923.

Carson Agency. Carson Indian School, boxes 1–19, 28.

Carson Indian School. Administrative Files, 1909–1923, boxes 262, 270–73.

Nevada General Records of Agency and Non-agency Indian Groups, 1908–1926, boxes 10–14.

Records of the Special Agent at Large (Reno). Investigative Records—Colonel L. A. Dorrington, 1913–1923, boxes 1–15.

Walker River Agency Correspondence. Walker River Agency Correspondence, 1906–1932, box 252.

Western Nevada Agency, Carson. Tribal Ops, Council Minutes/Resolutions 1940–74, boxes 7 and 8.

National Archives and Records Service, General Services Administration. Letters Received by the Office of Indian Affairs, 1824–81. Nevada Superintendency, 1861–80. National Archives Microfilm Publications, microcopy 234, rolls 538–44. Washington, D.C.: National Archives and Records Service, General Services Administration, 1959.

University of Nevada, Reno. Special Collections Department, Getchell Library.

Warren d'Azevedo Papers. Collection 97-04, box 6.

Warren L. d'Azevedo Washo Indians Research Papers. Collection 99-39, box 2.

Edgar E. Siskin Papers. Collection 90-68, box 1.

George F. Wright. Washoe Claims Case Records. Collection 90-37/1.

PUBLISHED PRIMARY SOURCES

Annual Report of the Commissioner of Indian Affairs. Washington, D.C.: Government Printing Office, 1848–1917.

Frémont, John C. *Narratives of Explorations and Adventure.* Edited by Allan Nevins. New York: Longmans, Green, 1956.

Jones and Stokes Associates, Inc. *Cave Rock Management Plan Final Environmental Impact Statement.* Sacramento, Calif.: Jones and Stokes, 2002.

King, R. T. *Contribution to a Survey of Life in Carson Valley, 1850s–1950s.* Reno: Oral History Program, University of Nevada, Reno Library, University of Nevada System, 1984.

NEWSPAPERS

Chicago Sun Times (Chicago, Illinois).

High Country News (Paonia, Colorado).

Las Vegas Sun (Las Vegas, Nevada)

Los Angeles Times (Los Angeles, California).

Record Courier (Gardnerville, Nevada).

San Francisco Chronicle (San Francisco, California).

San Francisco Herald (San Francisco, California).

Tahoe Daily Tribune (South Lake Tahoe, California).

Tahoe Bonanza (Tahoe City, California).

Secondary Sources

Anderson, M. K. *Tending the Wild: Native American Knowledge and the Management of California's Natural Resources.* Berkeley: University of California Press, 2005.

D'Azevedo, Warren L. "Washoe." In *The Handbook of North American Indians,* vol. 11, ed. William Sturtevant, 466–96. Washington, D.C.: Smithsonian Institution, 1986.

———. "The Washo Indians of California and Nevada." *University of Utah Anthropological Papers* 67 (May 1963): 1–25.

———. "The Washoe People in the Twentieth Century." Paper presented to the Third Annual Wa-She-Shu-Edu, Festival of Native American Arts and Culture at Tallac Historic Site, Lake Tahoe, California, July 30, 1993.

Basso, Keith H. *Wisdom Sits in Places: Landscape and Language among the Western Apache.* Albuquerque: University of New Mexico Press, 1996.

Berger, Thomas R. *A Long and Terrible Shadow: White Values, Native Rights in the Americas since 1492.* Seattle: University of Washington Press, 1992.

Berkhofer, Robert F. Jr. *The White Man's Indian: Images of the Indian from Columbus to the Present.* New York: Alfred A. Knopf, 1977.

Burton, Lloyd. *Worship and Wilderness: Culture, Religion, and Law in the Management of Public Lands and Resources.* Madison: University of Wisconsin Press, 2002.

Carville, Mike. *Rock Climbing Lake Tahoe.* Helena, Mt.: Falcon Books, 1999.

Davis, Sam P., ed. *The History of Nevada.* Reno: Elms Publishing, 1913.

Deloria, Vine Jr. *The Metaphysics of Modern Existence.* San Francisco: Harper and Row, 1979.

———. "Out of Chaos." In *I Become Part of It,* ed. D. M. Dooling and Paul Jordon Smith. New York: Parabola Books, 1989.

———. *Spirit and Reason: The Vine Deloria, Jr., Reader.* Golden, Colo.: Fulcrum Publishing, 1999.

Downs, James F. *The Two Worlds of the Washo, an Indian Tribe of California and Nevada.* New York: Holt, Rhinehart and Winston, 1966.

———. "Washo Religion." *University of California Publications: Anthropological Records* 16, no. 9 (1960): 370–92.

Fixico, Donald L. *The Invasion of Indian Country in the Twentieth Century: American Capitalism and Tribal Natural Resources.* Niwot: University Press of Colorado, 1998.

Ford, Susan Wise. "Lorenzo D. Creel and the Purchase of Land for Washoe Colonies, 1917." Master's thesis, University of Nevada, Reno, 1989.

Freed, Ruth, and Stanley Freed. "A Configuration of Aboriginal Washoe Culture." In *The Washoe Indians of California and Nevada,* ed. Warren L. d'Azevedo, 42–56. Salt Lake City: University of Utah Press–Anthropology Publications, 1963.

"Geographical Record." *Geographical Review* 18, no. 2 (1928): 321–35.

Grijalva, Therese C., Robert P. Berrens, Alok K. Bohara, Paul M. Jakus, and W. Doulass Shaw. "Valuing the Loss of Rock Climbing Access in Wilderness Areas: A National-Level, Random-Utility Model." *Land Economics* 78, no. 1 (2002): 103–20.

Hagan, William T. "United States Indian Policies, 1860–1900." In *The Handbook of North American Indians* 8, ed. William C. Sturtevant, 51–65. Washington, D.C.: Smithsonian Institution, 1986.

Hamilton, Lawrence C. "Modern American Rock: Some Aspects of Social Change." *Pacific Sociological Review* 22, no. 3 (1979): 285–308.

Handelman, Don. "Aspects of the Moral Compact of a Washo Shaman." *Anthropological Quarterly* 45, no. 2 (1972): 84–98.

———. "The Development of a Washo Shaman." In *Native Californians: A Theoretical Retrospective,* ed. John Lowell Bean and Thomas Blackburn, 379–407. Socorro, N.M.: Ballena Press, 1976.

———. "Trans-cultural Shamanic Healing: A Washoe Example." *Ethnos* 32 (1967): 149–66.

Heizer, Robert, and Albert B. Elsasser. "Some Archaeological Sites and Cultures of the Central Sierra Nevada." *University of California Archaeological Survey Reports* 21 (1953): 1–42.

Herz, Richard. "Legal Protection for Indigenous Cultures: Sacred Sites and Communal Rights." *Virginia Law Review* 79, no. 3 (1993): 691–716.

"Hot Flashes." *Climbing*, no. 132 (June–July 1992).

Howard, Thomas Frederick. *Sierra Crossing: First Roads to California*. Berkeley: University of California Press, 1998.

Hoxie, Frederick E. *A Final Promise: The Campaign to Assimilate the Indians, 1880–1920*. Lincoln: University of Nebraska Press, 1984.

Hurtado, Albert L. *Indian Survival on the California Frontier.* New Haven: Yale University Press, 1988.

———. *John Sutter: A Life on the North American Frontier.* Norman: University of Oklahoma Press, 2006.

Hurtado, Albert L., and Peter Iverson, eds. *Major Problems in American Indian History.* Lexington, Mass.: D. C. Heath, 1994.

Iverson, Peter. *"We Are Still Here": American Indians in the Twentieth Century.* Wheeling: Harlan Davidson, 1998. American History Series.

Kappler, Charles J., ed. *Indian Affairs Laws and Treaties.* Vol. 4: *(Laws) Compiled to March 4, 1927*. Washington, D.C.: Government Printing Office, 1919.

Knack, Martha C. *Boundaries Between: The Southern Paiutes, 1775–1995*. Lincoln: University of Nebraska Press.

Knack, Martha C., and Omer Stewart. *As Long as the Rivers Shall Run: An Ethnohistory of the Pyramid Lake Paiute*. Berkeley: University of California Press, 1984.

Kroeber, Alfred Louis. "Cultural and Natural Areas of Native North America." *University of California Publications in American Archaeology and Ethnology* 38 (1947): 1–242.

———. "The Washo Language of East Central California and Nevada." *University of California Publications in American Archaeology and Ethnology* 4, no. 5 (1907): 251–318.

Lewis, David Rich. "Native Americans in the 19th-Century West." In *A Companion to the American West*, ed. William Deverell, 143–62. Malden, Mass.: Blackwell, 2004.

Limerick, Patricia Nelson. *The Legacy of Conquest: The Unbroken Past of the American West*. New York: W. W. Norton, 1987.

Lowie, Robert H. "Ethnographic Notes on the Washo." *University of California Publications in American Archaeology and Ethnology* 36, no. 5 (1939): 301–52.

———. "Washo Texts." *Publication of the Archives of Languages of the World* (Anthropology Department, Indiana University) 5, no. 7 (1963): 1–30.

Michaelsen, Robert S. "American Indian Religious Freedom Litigation: Promise and Perils." *Journal of Law and Religion* 3, no. 1 (1985): 47–76.

Nabokov, Peter. *A Forest of Time: American Indian Ways of History.* Cambridge: Cambridge University Press, 2002.

———. *Where the Lightning Strikes: The Lives of American Indian Sacred Places.* New York: Penguin Group, Viking, 2006.

Nevers, Jo Ann. *Wa She Shu: A Washo Tribal History.* Reno: Inter-tribal Council of Nevada, 1976.

"Notes and News." *American Antiquity* 23, no. 3 (1958): 330–44.

Obermayr, Erich. *Foot Path to Four-Lane: A Historical Guidebook to Transportation on Lake Tahoe's Southeast Shore.* Moundhouse, Nev.: Nevada Department of Transportation, 2005.

Ogburn, William F. "Inventions and Discoveries." *American Journal of Sociology* 34, no. 1 (1928): 25–39.

Paxson, Frederic L. "The Highway Movement, 1916–1935." *American Historical Review* 51, no. 2 (1946): 236–53.

Prucha, Francis P., ed. *Documents of United States Indian Policy.* 2d ed. Lincoln: University of Nebraska Press, 1990.

———. *The Great Father: The United States Government and the American Indians.* 2 vols. Lincoln: University of Nebraska Press, 1984.

Rossiter, Richard. *Rock Climbing the Flatirons.* Guilford, Conn.: Globe Pequot, 1999.

Rowley, William D. *Reclaiming the Arid West: The Career of Francis Newlands.* Bloomington: Indiana University Press, 1996.

Sarris, Greg. *Mabel Mckay: Weaving the Dream.* Berkeley: University of California Press, 1994.

Scott, Edward B. *The Saga of Lake Tahoe.* Vol. 1. Crystal Bay, Nev.: Sierra-Tahoe Publishing, 1957.

———. *The Saga of Lake Tahoe.* Vol. 2. Crystal Bay, Nev.: Sierra-Tahoe Publishing, 1973.

Siskin, Edgar. *Washo Shamans and Peyotists: Religious Conflict in an American Indian Tribe.* Salt Lake City: University of Utah Press, 1983.

Sproul, David Kent. *A Bridge between Cultures: An Administrative History of Rainbow Bridge National Monument.* Denver: National Park Service, 2001.

State of Nevada. *Eighth Biennial Report of the Department of Highways: For the Period December 1, 1930 to June 30, 1932, Inclusive.* Carson City: State Printing Office, 1932.

Strong Douglas H. *Tahoe: An Environmental History.* Lincoln: University of Nebraska Press, 1984.

Szasz, Margaret Connell. *Education and the American Indian: The Road to Self-*

Determination since 1928. 3rd ed. Albuquerque: University of New Mexico Press, 1999.

Todhunter, Andrew. *Fall of the Phantom Lord.* New York: Doubleday, 1998.

———. "The Precipitous World of Dan Osman." *Atlantic Monthly* 277, no. 2 (1996): 98–105.

Unruh, John D. Jr. *The Plains Across: The Overland Emigrants and the Trans-Mississippi West, 1840–1860.* Urbana: University of Illinois Press, 1979.

Vitebsky, Piers. *Shamanism.* New York: Little, Brown, 1995. Reprint. Norman: University of Oklahoma Press, 2001.

Wilkinson, Charles. *Blood Struggle: The Rise of Modern Indian Nations.* New York: W. W. Norton, 2005.

Yablon, Marcia. "Property Rights and Sacred Sites: Federal Regulatory Responses to American Indian Religious Claims on Public Land." *Yale Law Journal* 113, no. 7 (2004): 1623–62.

INDEX